Forty-fied

Forty-fied

How to Be a Fortysomething

Malcolm Burgess

ICON BOOKS

Published in the UK in 2007 by
Icon Books Ltd, The Old Dairy,
Brook Road, Thriplow,
Cambridge SG8 7RG
email: info@iconbooks.co.uk
www.iconbooks.co.uk

Sold in the UK, Europe, South Africa and Asia
by Faber & Faber Ltd, 3 Queen Square,
London WC1N 3AU or their agents

Distributed in the UK, Europe, South Africa and Asia
by TBS Ltd, TBS Distribution Centre, Colchester Road,
Frating Green, Colchester CO7 7DW

This edition published in Australia in 2007
by Allen & Unwin Pty Ltd,
PO Box 8500, 83 Alexander Street,
Crows Nest, NSW 2065

Distributed in Canada by
Penguin Books Canada,
90 Eglinton Avenue East, Suite 700,
Toronto, Ontario M4P 2YE

ISBN: 978-1840468-23-6

Typeset in 11 on 14 pt Gill Sans by Wayzgoose

Printed and bound in the UK by J.H. Haynes & Co. Ltd

To Heather ...
and my therapist,
for everything.

Malcolm Burgess, 49, is a journalist, author and scriptwriter. His comic series have appeared in *The Times*, the *Mail on Sunday's You* magazine, the *Evening Standard*, the *Financial Times*, the *Guardian*, and *Metro*, in which *I Hate the Office*, his recent best-selling book, was originally a weekly column.

One day we're normal and reasonably functioning members of society. The next we're neurotic, raging paranoids who don't know if we should be congratulated, commiserated with or just humanely locked up out of sight in a nice, tasteful Mrs Rochester loft conversion. Congratulations: it's our fortieth birthday – or the 'Big FOUR-O', as everyone likes to tell us in deliberately loud stage whispers. They wouldn't like anybody not to know how grotesquely old and mockable we are. Welcome to the scary Big Person's World.

It's made more confusing because being in our forties isn't what it was. Thirty years ago when our parents were the same age they seemed to know exactly what was expected of them and to do it much better. They didn't see Middle Age as a death sentence but as an opportunity to get down and dirty with their herbaceous borders and to save wool. It was their turn to pass on the baton to the next generation – not to hang around Top Shop and scare teenage customers into thinking they were store detectives.

The problem is that, today, we lack convincing role-models and no one's quite sure what acting your age at forty is any more. Is it about constantly re-inventing yourself like Madonna? Is it about still buying enough CDs to personally keep HMV solvent? Is it about feeling that shop assistants are ruder and that graffiti artists should at least learn to spell 'fuck'?

Blame the sixties. Blame the 'have it all' eighties. Blame everyone's rising expectations. Blame greater equality. It's not really surprising that we're the generation that can't decide if we should be wowing them in the office or concentrating our efforts on being good parents – a conflict of interests that can lead to hoping no one notices that our shepherd in the school Nativity is wearing an unwashed John Lewis tea towel.

Because to be a fortysomething now is, literally, to be everything. We're parents, step-parents, parents of second families, singletons, co-habitees, grandparents. We're battling with babies, Bratz-crazed teenies and moody teenagers. We're working 24/7. We're being told we can still wear unsuitably youthful clothes and enjoy the White Stripes. We're still having lots of sex of course – as befits the generation that likes to think it put the Joy into it. In fact, we're behaving in a thoroughly confusing and embarrassing way to both a younger and older generation. It's not surprising they'd much prefer it if we did some proper housework and home maintenance, as is our true destiny, and stopped making those funny movements while humming Cold-play songs.

Of course, few forties have intentions of passing on any batons yet. Though this isn't to say that we can't see the attractions of having long, restful, non-child-oriented holidays that don't involve ours going down a flume in a Center Parc in February 1,894 times. And there are unquestionably things we know by our forties – about life, love, death and the correct plural of phenomenon – that make those in their twenties and thirties seem positively callow in comparison.

Middle age? Mid-youth? The beginning of wisdom? The beginning of botox? Most of us would just say plain bloody knackered actually and leave it at that.

A

Acceptable Amnesia or Things Every Forty-something is Allowed to Forget Sometimes

Forty-eight of their fifty passwords, including their mother's maiden name.

Their child, who is currently standing outside the school gates.

Council bin-men work by the non-Gregorian calendar.

A pet's birthday.

Part of their shopping.

Any recipe that doesn't include pasta.

They have a brain.

Their name.

Advertising

While your age group, together with baby boomers, forms a burgeoning and wealthy part of the population, it's noticeable how rarely advertising reflects your real world, or even deigns to acknowledge your actual existence.

People in their forties largely seem to drop off the media horizon, like lemmings in some mass suicidal purge, whereby only the young and beautiful and a few intrepid OAPs in tea bag ads are allowed to remain. You realise you're no longer aspirational or obviously attractive, but you would sometimes like to see yourself represented as more than:

- A dangerous driver who runs over a lollipop lady, but thanks to an accident claim is able to sue her and go on a cruise.

- A business person in a meeting who finds his life transformed by a Quality Solution that no one understands.

- A farmer from the developing world whose name begins with the same first letter as his identically sized produce specially grown for a supermarket, and who is ecstatically happy about being paid very little for this.

- A well-known celebrity promoting a cut-price supermarket chain, who in real life wouldn't venture beyond Marylebone High Street.

- Someone who in real life obviously doesn't have grey hair but, we are led to believe, finds his ideal 'natural' colour, together with a much younger half-dressed woman, although it is not clear if she comes free with the bottle or not.

- A smug drinker of hot chocolate who wears permanent comfy slippers and a snooze suit sitting on a nasty velour sofa, and whose face everyone wants to smash in.

Advice

For whatever reason, not a lot of good advice ever seems to come the fortysomethings' way. It's true that we get a certain amount of advice from the young, chiefly that we're embarrassing in public places and shouldn't speak above a whisper ever again, and will never, ever understand the plot of 24 so it's not even worth trying. But we know this already, bless, although it's always nice of them to remind us. It's advice from the older generation, on the other hand, that is scarier and seems designed to confuse us totally.

> Your father and I had separate beds once we were forty. You won't be able to drag yourselves apart from each other at this age.

Children are exhausting and you can expect to be in bed by 8.30pm every evening.
Children give you a new lease of life.

You'll have to move to Sevenoaks.
Never leave London if you want to see a non-multiplex film ever again.

You need to wear a colour that matches your skin tone, hair colour and personality, i.e. beige.
There's no law that says you shouldn't wear a top Amy Winehouse would find shocking.

You should be driving a Volvo.
Go on, it will be your last chance to see if you can try and break the land speed record.

You won't want to jeopardise your pension by moving jobs at your age.
Life's a risk, so what have you got to lose?

If you're a woman you can't possibly juggle work and family life.
Unless you use your brain, you're going to become one of those sad people shouting out the wrong answers to *Countdown*.

Affair

While full-blown affairs are not unknown among this age group, it is worth considering if a twenty-second liaison on the photocopier at the office Christmas party can truly be said to be an affair and not just another sad and desultory experience of finding the toner cartridge is empty again.

More interesting in French movies, where everyone over forty is expected to have a slightly angst-ridden one, and not to like wearing clothes, especially if they are played by Emmanuelle Béart.

Ageism

Once you hit your forties no one will ever see you in the same way again. It's as if overnight part of you exits and comes back metamorphosed into Dot Cotton's only slightly younger sibling. That's why, come the Big Four-O, everyone will assume you're going to be totally incapable of:

- Having a good business idea ever again.

- Successfully operating a PC or anything that involves electricity.

- Appearing in a major Hollywood film if you're a woman, unless it's someone's (a) mother; (b) grandmother; (c) freakish boss.

- Having a zeitgeist moment, because the latter has well and truly passed you by, loser.

It's not entirely clear in offices what age they'd ideally like everyone to be. Half of us are accused of being too young and inexperienced and lacking in basic skills; the other half are being subtly or not so subtly reminded that our best years of faxing are behind us and maybe a customer care post in B&Q advising on avocado bathroom suites would suit our mature skills better.

But, at the end of the day, you may need to ask yourself: do I really need to resort to a range of strategies from lying to having botox and plastic surgery in order to let everyone know that I am desperate and over forty and don't mind questions from the confused birthday party organiser about what age I actually want to be. Or have I reached the age I am with a modicum of wise detachment and benign self-knowledge as I become an Ambassador for the New Aquarian Age? Er, you choose.

Agent Provocateur

It's seriously not only for mistresses – every fortysomething woman would like one item of inappropriate sexy lingerie for a birthday or Christmas present, just for once please. Even if they know the bra will be left at the back of a drawer and will only be worn by a child doing a Madonna impersonation or used as an emergency bird feeder.

Ailments

You're quite likely to be afflicted by a wide range of new ailments, physical and psychological, all of which can be traced to your advancing years. The good news is that most can easily be cured by a brisk walk and never watching *Desperate Housewives* ever again.

Festival Ear: Condition chiefly brought about by not having attended a rock festival for over twenty years. Early signs include the comment 'why is the music so loud? I don't remember it being this ear-splitting when we were playing our nose flutes at Glastonbury in 1983. What's wrong with today's young people?'

Texter's Finger: That funny way people over forty text, as if it might be dangerous to exceed two letters a minute, is a condition that is only likely to worsen over time and is best dealt with in the comfort of the sufferer's own bedroom, where at least no one can make any more smart-arse comments.

Mistaken Identity: Potentially serious condition by which you believe you are actually much younger than you are. Ages can range from early thirties to as young as six, and can be brought on by a wide range of triggers from a quick lunchtime botox to someone telling you you'd like *Second Life*.

Dad-dancing: Male urge to flail limbs uncontrollably as if actually performing dance movements; usually reaches peak during Paul Weller's 'Wildwood'. Fortunately often more distressing for the bystander than the sufferer himself.

Phantom Limbs: Affects many men who can often feel one or both legs scoring the epoch-defying winning goal at the Cup Final, even though they themselves were rejected for the works team on the grounds of apparently having two artificial left feet.

Temporary Blindness: Traumatic condition usually brought on by sudden visit to an H&M and, even though it is a typical English summer, buying items that even Kate Moss might find too embarrassing.

Senior Moments: We're sure you'd prefer to draw a veil over this one. If you can even remember where you put it, that is.

Alienated, Of Course You Are

Not quite in the teenage sense of 'why is everyone against me and why can't I leave school now and be a graffiti artist?', but more in the sense of 'who invented the annual season ticket and is there a sun oil franchise on Marbella beach with convenient hut I could live in please? Now.'

All-nighters

Post-tiredness hallucinations, wet clothes requiring frequent changes, a belief that a clean nappy would solve everyone's problems, touching something very sticky and unmentionable, and the search for a new wonder drug offering universal peace and love. Those all-night raves in fields of yore singing 'Sorted for Es and Whizz' may have more in common with life today than you might first have thought. But why the long face? 'The Wheels on the Bus Go Round and Round' is a perfectly good song: sung with a certain edge at 2.30 am, it might be trying to tell us something.

Chris and Beth, the couple who always wanted to be in their forties

Chris and Beth had always wanted to be in their forties. It was their platonic age. They were the only people anyone knew, outside a developing world country where the average life expectancy was thirty-seven, who positively welcomed being in their fifth decade.

It was just a shame they hadn't met earlier. It would have saved both of them an awful lot of anxiety to be with someone else who didn't know what techno trance was either or why everyone giggled when 69 was mentioned. They had both tried in different ways to be young, but it hadn't really worked. Chris was always the person in the disco who wore mail order catalogue clothes one size too big, couldn't dance and ended up discussing the Heimlich Technique with the only adult present. Beth grew up always being the odd one out at parties and falling asleep under piles of coats in bedrooms, where at least she was comfortably hidden.

It was their joint passion for Esperanto that had brought them together at university. Neither knew where it had come from, but it was a well spring with seemingly illimitable depths. They had both joined the university group and their intimacy had been sealed (admittedly not very difficult when there was only one other member who left soon after). They were both dedicated to the movement's ambitious ideals of one universal language to bring the world's warring populations together, followed by a world government, while appreciating that there was still some way to go for everyone concerned. At least their children would have something nice and concrete to sigh at and lose their eyeballs at the backs of their heads over, people had said at their wedding, and it would be useful for when they wanted to talk about sex at home. Their parents had to dissuade them from having the service in Esperanto, but anyone who listened carefully might have heard something resembling Klingon during the final vows.

Everyone said that your children add years to your appearance and they had both been secretly excited by this. In any case, they were much too busy to care, with their growing family, and as joint secretary and treasurer of the only remaining Esperanto group in Hertfordshire (there were no other members), not to forget Beth's sterling work coaching Girl Guides for their Esperanto badge.

It was in their thirties – which all their friends dreaded because of the decade that followed – that they seemed to blossom further. They thought that things couldn't get better, but they could. They must have been the only people who weren't checking for signs of imminent middle-age and dressing inappropriately as if they were wearing big signs saying 'Hi, I'm 39 and I thought I'd draw attention to myself and my low self-esteem by wearing this ludicrous top.' Beth had been invited to a fun sex-toy party by her friends, but asked if she could be let off wearing her female orgasm balls and sell them as big marbles for her Girl Guide money raiser.

Of course, now they were both forty, Chris and Beth felt ecstatic. It wasn't a mute or gradual acceptance either – theirs was a lock, stock and barrel 'YES', not waving or drowning, but doing a full-bodied and sensible breast stroke into the years ahead. Even their parents wondered where they had gone wrong and if there shouldn't be a stage before you wore a practical navy blue fleece for the rest of your life. Needless to say, Chris and Beth weren't reading *Uncut*, wearing the same pair of jeans as their children or offering them embarrassing intimate advice, and had never once thought about plastic surgery.

If it was all downhill from here on, they looked like the only ones who would be properly dressed to enjoy the ride. They were boldly going where no one since Janet and John's parents had gone before. It was a release, a letting go. And elasticated leisure trousers definitely helped, there was no question.

Americana

Faux country and western music, whose moaning songs about unsuccessful love, depression and bleak prairie landscapes seem to strike a chord with fortysomething men who wouldn't normally be seen dead listening to Tammy Wynette. Some see it as a cry for help – though this could also be coming from their partners, who claim that Leonard Cohen is a ray of sunshine in comparison, quite honestly.

Amis, Martin

Formerly 'angry young man' of English letters and writer of novels like *London Fields* and *Money*, which helped sum up our eighties zeitgeist. But then had a lot of trouble with his teeth, got divorced and failed to be nominated for the Booker Prize. Many fortysomethings are able to sympathise and make a direct comparison with their own unfortunate lives, although in most cases they wouldn't blame Julian Barnes or Zadie Smith.

Angst

For some reason forty seems to attract more personal anxiety than turning thirty or fifty – made worse by friends and colleagues doing their utmost to ensure that no potential embarrassment or humiliation is left unturned. After all, when else will they have the opportunity to buy you a gift-wrapped Rampant Rabbit from Ann Summers that will start moving about on the bus, together with maximum seepage from your Love Oil, despite your protestations to fellow passengers that it's only a highly charged mobile phone? If nothing else, at least you'll have a spare seat next to you.

Aniston, Jennifer

Nearly forty, a fabulous TV career, some decent films and a multi-millionairess ... Nearly forty, a series of failed relationships and no children.

Only you know how jealous, bitter and twisted you're feeling today.

Anti-ageing Cosmetics

While for the under-thirties these winsomely offer themselves as maybe useful protection for the nasty storms ahead, come forty they let you know loudly and clearly that if you're not slathered to the *n*th degree in unattractive oily gunk at most times of the day, only dropping dead might make you feel better.

To make it extra traumatic for you, celebrities like Andie MacDowell or Kristin Scott Thomas – who may even be depressingly older than you – insist on reminding you that you're 'worth it'. This is just in case you're having any qualms about applying to your person something that came from a shark's foreskin – and costs the equivalent of the GDP of a minor developing nation.

But unfortunately looking like a North Sea trawler fisherman with a fake tan isn't an option for most women, who will succumb sooner or later and try not to get too depressed when someone takes them aside and says 'Nivea' to them sternly. Male fortysomethings, by the way, usually appear in adverts as dire warnings of what happens if you don't moisturise or exfoliate regularly and are seen as lost to the metrosexual cause for ever.

Antiques Road Show, The

The litmus test of advancing middle age. Best to sell your Spodewear sugar bowl on e-Bay if you can, and avoid being publicly humiliated as the person who used it to keep the rabbits' rectal thermometer in for twelve years.

Archers, The

While listening occasionally, preferably by accident, is regarded as permissible, having a regular appointment is tantamount to saying 'I have become well and truly middle-aged and will soon be dreaming about Melvyn Bragg and know the correct height for a *Cupressus leylandii*.'

Putting the omnibus edition on for a special treat suggests that Sunday mornings are no longer for sleeping off those wild Saturday nights of your youth – or that you really don't have anything else better to do. Humming the theme tune and buying the board game suggest yours is a truly terminal condition.

Attitudes

Some of us actually don't mind being forty. Well, not to begin with, that is. It's only once we start considering other people's attitudes – and talking to other fortysomethings – that we start wondering whether we should just go and ask someone to put us right out of our misery.

You: Don't worry, you're as old as you feel.

Friend: Thanks, I feel about a hundred.

You: Do you remember when there was that TV series and it was glamorous to be a thirtysomething? The producers obviously thought they were being daring and innovative, with characters who did a lot of lying by log fires and talking about their issues.

Friend: There wasn't a sequel though, was there: the 'Tissue's in My Fleece Pocket And Don't Use Your Finger' Years?

You: There was *Sex and the City*.

Friend: Oh, God, so like our lives.

You: I suppose there was *Friends*, with the cast in their late thirties.

Friend: Behaving like people in their twenties. The actors couldn't have carried on in their forties – they'd have died of terminal cuteness. No wonder it had to end. We're the demographic that everyone is rather embarrassed about, a generation without a name.

You: There was that Caroline Quentin series on ITV.

Friend: Oh, God, everyone wore anoraks and looked grumpy. At least they got to wear Manolo Blahniks on *Sex and the City*.

You: When actually we're all very different, have a lot of varied life experience, can sense a teenage request for money at a hundred paces and had the eighties as our form-ative decade.

Friend: But everybody hates the eighties and says it was just about profit and greed. That's not exactly going to help our self-esteem, is it?

You: There's always Madonna.

Friend: She always comes up.

You: She is forty-nine and the most successful and richest female singer in music history who's constantly re-inventing herself.

Friend: Except everyone then starts making comparisons and you're always pig slops.

You: I thought we were supposed to be the new thirty any-way?

Friend: I don't think I want to be. It sounds too exhausting.

You: So you're glad to be forty?

Friend: I didn't say that.

You: You know, I think I might have come up with a definition for what it is to be forty.

Friend: You have?

You: We're not thirty and we're not fifty.

Friend: Why didn't I think of that? What a concept! I feel better already, thank you very much.

B

Baby Boomers

Whether it's Bill Clinton doing his post-Presidential thing, or Helen Mirren winning Oscars, we can't help but hear what a fabulous time the 'Sixties' generation is having.

In fact, everywhere we turn we're hearing about how they're entitled to unlimited sex, not necessarily with the same partner, overdose on HRT, spend their children's inheritance whichever hedonistic way they like, and are able to retire early on a proper final pension scheme, while reminding you that without their generation there would be no feminism, gay rights or multi-culturalism.

You, in return, can look forward to working for ever, having a poorer pension, if any, paying for your children's university education and realising you'll be about ninety when your mortgage is finally paid. It's hardly surprising that you have a rather sclerotic inner dialogue blaming yourself for not having been born at least twenty years earlier and sticking some flowers in your hair.

After all, you will probably be accused of being a baby boomer by your children, commenting resentfully on all the money you are wasting on such inessentials as having more than one pair of shoes, for example. Will evidence of your clapped out 1989 foot spa bought on e-Bay convince them that you're truly and utterly skint? Or maybe just remind them that they're never going to have a lunch in this town that isn't a basic Margherita with no extra toppings ever again.

Bad Back

Everyone will want to know if yours is a result of attempting really exciting and unusual sexual positions too extreme even to appear in the *Kama Sutra*. Try and retain your mystery for as long as you are able.

Baldness

Many terms about baldness, like the condition itself, try their best to cover up the problem. From 'slightly receding' to 'looking distinguished', there are a range of euphemisms to make every bald person feel better or worse about themselves. What they're really saying, of course, is that 'you're a slap head and it does seem a bit sad kidding yourself like that, doesn't it?'

The 'being positive' attitude about baldness also includes hairdressers who, rather than lose half their clientele, are able to give customers amusing phantom haircuts and charge for them.

For a long time, a bald person's 'Number One' shaved haircut was known as a 'Grant', after the Ross Kemp character on EastEnders. Five minutes in the chair and the removal of a few extant hairs would usually set the sitter back a minimum of ten pounds. But the illusion that what was being done to your head could actually be called something certainly added to the bald person's self-esteem and went some way to convincing him that he could still operate as a person of hair in our hairist society. Unfortunately Kemp's departure from *EastEnders* and immersion in SAS roles hasn't led to many requests for 'that cute shaved look Ross Kemp has when he's eviscerating enemy agents'.

Men are advised that baldness runs in families, and that if your father or grandfathers were bald there's a good chance you will be mistaken for Iain Duncan-Smith from quite an early age. The clear message is that it's your DNA, sorry, and there's nothing you can do about it. And the sooner everyone accepts that, the better.

If, however, you are determined to remain among the ranks

of the haired, you are basically given two alternatives. You can go for the 'I want to look like Frank Sinatra and have expensive hair transplants so that everyone knows I'm going bald and feel very insecure about it' look. Or else you can go for the 'Elton John Special: has my hair been restored or is it just a bad wig day? You tell me' look. It's just a question of deciding which one will work most humiliatingly for you.

Nice people, usually one's partner, like to help by coming up with a list of all the attractive famous bald people in history, from William Shakespeare to Socrates (although this list does seem to peter out depressingly quickly). A list of all the attractive famous people with hair in history is never proffered, lest it lead to further feelings of low self-esteem. You can't help feeling that the list of non-attractive and non-famous bald people in history is probably best forgotten for the time being.

Other nice people, OK usually one's partner again, remind you that baldness is a result of above-average testosterone. You're actually super-sexed and abnormally virile, if this is any compensation. The suggestion that Billy Zane is in his forties and has a celebrity girlfriend who appeared on *Big Brother* is actually supposed to make you feel good about yourself, by the way.

If you don't know someone who can talk you up, then you may just have to say something reassuringly upbeat to yourself. Tell yourself that you don't mind being an emergency dog salt lick. Or remind yourself philosophically that, after all, someone's got to come between seagull droppings and the ground, and it might as well be you.

'Ballad of Lucy Jordan, The'

As we may recall, Marianne Faithful let us know about this poor woman who grew depressed because, at the age of thirty-seven, she'd never driven through Paris in a sports car with the warm wind through her hair. But, as any fortysomething more attuned to fortune's slings and arrows will remind her, it won't take her long to pull herself together, accept suffering humbly and come up with a perfectly viable alternative – like a family holiday exploring the Travelodges of eastern Belgium. There's always a silver lining in every fortysomething's cloud.

Barbecues

It is expected that sooner or later the forties man will wish to purchase a barbecue. By succumbing to his 'inner sausage-pricker', he is answering a call that lies deep in the male psyche to have a burning pyre in his own back garden and to wear a plastic-bra-and-panties apron. After all, if he can no longer hunt, kill and maim, he can do the next best thing and perform violent acts upon a piece of marinated meat surrounded by his neighbours. This is, of course, provided he can actually light the barbecue and (a) it doesn't rain; (b) the Force 11 gale subsides; (c) none of the vegetarians present will mind a nice bit of Angus steak.

Everyone compliments him on his ability to successfully burn food, while his partner, who has done the family cooking for twenty years and never received any praise, is a little put out and suggests he might like to try bringing his 'transferable skills' into the kitchen. Everyone breathes a sigh of relief when he watches Ray Mears, and the barbecue becomes the new rockery as he moves on to roasting hedgehogs on a bonfire.

Barbie

'Nobody told me being forty was going to be like this.

Like most of my sorority, I wasn't looking too far into the future at that Hollywood High School graduation in 1978. Of course, I had always been quite mature for my years and people (I think we mean men here and unfortunately some feminists who should have known better) have often treated me as a sexual stereotype. People who know me would vouch that I was just an ordinary young Californian woman who had read Germaine Greer's The Female Eunuch *and realised she didn't have much to worry about in that department.*

But having graduated in Tennis Party Studies with Double Honours, like many of my peers I was faced with a plethora of choices about what I should be doing with the rest of my life. These included:

- *Coffee morning hostess*
- *Ballerina*
- *Doctor*
- *McDonald's worker*
- *Pilot*
- *Circus star*
- *Rock star*
- *Cheer leader*
- *Dinner party hostess*
- *Yoga instructor*
- *Astronaut*
- *Fashion model*
- *President*
- *Shopper*
- *Movie star*

What was I supposed to do? It's not really surprising that I decided to sample every one of them in my attempts to Have It All. This made it especially tough as, back in the eighties, we were being told by Shirley 'Superwoman' Conran that life was too short to stuff a mushroom but, on the other hand, it seemed to be the order of the day at all of the soignée dinner parties I was meant to hold. At least being a famous astronaut enabled me to escape from this at times.

My boyfriend Ken and I had an on-off relationship for a number of years. He had asked me to marry him on several occasions, but the time had never felt right. Besides I was doing well in my chosen multiple careers and didn't wish to be primarily known as The Person Who Washes Ken's Lumberjack Shirt and Chinos. To be perfectly honest, as an extra in Dynasty (he was a waiter at Blake Carrington's parties and once got to touch Joan Collins' shoulder pad), Ken wasn't earning a lot, and all my various salaries did create a certain imbalance in our relationship. We parted in 1996 when Ken went off into the Sierra Nevada to explore his 'crisis of masculinity' and discover his 'Inner Stetson', only slightly marred by his claim that I had lesbian tendencies.

I'd always been close to my nieces and nephews and, although I hadn't discounted the idea of having children, with my extensive career portfolio and the long hours worked, having a child would have been a disaster. I think I just followed the zeitgeist and it didn't seem to lead anywhere involving strawberry Calpol. But then it slowly dawned on me that my heroine Madonna – we're nearly the same age – already had two children and a new one recently flown in from Africa and there was something in my life that wasn't being satisfied even by my most recent career as US ambassador. I began dating again.

I am currently three months pregnant at the age of forty-eight and dreading telling my boss, who I just know will say that I'm the person who had to go and have sex and screw the whole company. I forgot to tell you that the father is Ken – we had a rapprochement. I did some speed dating and guess who was the first person who didn't hide in the toilet because he couldn't take the pressure of being a celebrity's boring partner? He is dreaming of organising a neighbourhood soccer team and owning a shed for the first time in his life. I am happy, I think, although worried that I won't have an outfit for 'Child Vomiting at Frequent Intervals That Will Also Have

To Be Worn in Business Meeting', but Ken thinks he may have an old fleece I can wear.'

BBC2

Apparently BBC2 is the TV station most likely to be viewed by the over-forties and quite honestly we're not surprised. But maybe don't tell anyone you turned over to watch *Meerkat Manor* because you thought (a) *The West Wing*, with its over-lapping dialogue, makes you think your hearing is going; (b) *Lost* is where your most cliched holiday nightmare ever meets *The Famous Five Have a Wonderful Adventure*; (c) *Big Brother* was the closest thing you had seen to the decline and fall of the Roman Empire since your last office Christmas party.

Being Confused

Can someone your age be arrested for going on MySpace? Which focus group from hell came up with the Bratz/Forever Diamondz Funky Torso? What's the point of flash mobbing and dancing around a furniture store with people you've never seen before? Don't worry, you're reaching the foothills or shallow waters of middle age. But just wait until you get to that bit with the warning sign that says 'From this point onwards you will never be able to watch most adverts, listen to most music or understand anything that appears on Channel 4 after nine o'clock in the evening ever again.' Plenty to look forward to then.

Being Surprised at What You Know

By the age of forty it's easy to believe your brain cells have atrophied and that on a bad day you make Jade Goody sound like Albert Einstein on steroids. But it's worth reminding yourself that you do in fact know a remarkable number of things, all completely unrelated and useless of course, but bound to impress any group of six-year-olds who are thinking of becoming pub quiz champions:

- The plural of 'phenomenon'.

- Every number one record from 1970 to 1980.

- The correct use of the apostrophe.

- The right 'its'.

- How to calculate swimming pool capacities on the basis of the number of saucepans of water needed.

- The rules for using a Bunsen burner.

- The creators of *Crossroads*.

- At least one medieval English monarch.

- The colours of the prism.

- The names of every Cup Final winner from 1985 to the present.

- At least six theories on what *The Magic Roundabout* is really meant to be about.

- How to address a Bishop.

- The correct use of 'sincerely' and 'faithfully' when writing unctuously to your bank manager about an overdraft.

Bestseller, Writing a

With numerous other glittering career possibilities having failed to materialise, writing sounds like a winner for many desperate forties people attracted by a lot of nice sitting down and being paid large sums of money at the end of it.

Whether it's because of the scientific theory that putting a group of monkeys in a room with a typewriter will eventually see them produce the works of Shakespeare or because many writers are unattractive, no one is quite sure. But there remains a firm conviction that there's a bestseller in every one of us. It's just a question of waiting and finding the right story about a boy brought up in a school for wizards, who then discovers a secret global conspiracy based on the writings of Leonardo da Vinci. Just don't rush it.

How to write good: have you got what it takes?

Queen's English: You should have a reasonable grasp of this. If not, do not worry unduly.

Action: Your (potential) bestseller must be packed with it. Who, after all, would want to spend an entire chapter setting the scene when the hero can be tortured, maimed and traumatised, have an affair with a psychic lesbian killer and discover a global conspiracy to take over the world all on the first page?

Explosive secret: If you have one of these, there must be three sisters who are respectively glamorous, powerful and talented, and among them share an 'explosive secret' not revealed until the last page. If you can't decide on the secret, hint at a forthcoming sequel or trilogy.

Bed: Never extraneous to the plot. Characters may lead active sex lives in explicit detail and have any number of unsuitable relationships, but only to develop the story. Usually toward the next bedroom.

Historical: Remember that thousands of years of human history are out of bounds. Little of significance occurred until the invention of the wimple and the assuaging of the critical shortage of taffeta and tulle with the Voyages of Discovery.

Identity: Unless an occasional wearer of tinted contact lenses, your hero or heroine should not have emerald eyes on one page and soft brown ones a few pages later. Your editor should feel he or she can broach the subject without you breaking down and claiming that no one treated Tolstoy like this.

The noughties: Our caring, environmental decade should prove no hindrance to a writer with a dynamic, entrepreneurial message. But watch out for flying lawsuits if recycling others' material.

Tinsel Town: You must remain ambiguous on the subject of Hollywood. On the one hand, it is a den of adultery, corruption, ruthlessness and coke-sniffing; on the other, it's a gift for a blockbuster author. On no account give the impression that modern Hollywood is geared solely to TV films and dog food commercials.

Fate: If you feel plotting is not your strong point, refer often to this subject to suggest your protagonist has little control of his or her path through life.

Aristos: You can never have enough of them. Should your creativity be flagging, there is nothing wrong with using real-life royals based on research from *Hello* magazine. If anyone ever claims your writing is unrealistic and two-dimensional, you can always get your own back and reveal your source.

Men: Are only interested in one thing and will love the heroine and leave her, although she will never learn.

X-rated: Those extra-spicy bits even you dare not mention; also the potentially libellous introductions of real characters, e.g. Prime Ministers, MPs, etc.

Zeitgeist: Make sure your characters reflect the true spirit of the age. But they shouldn't show off their BlackBerries on every page because it can get a bit boring.

Romance: Have you ever been in a vaguely romantic situation? Or maybe had something slightly funny happen to you? Then there's no reason on earth why you shouldn't be writing a romantic comedy – or 'rom-com' if you decide to sell the movie rights to a famous American movie star (or else straight to DVD with Minnie Driver).

Rom-com: Fortunately, with your book containing both romance and comedy, readers won't be expecting too much of either. If they happen to laugh and cry in the wrong places they can't blame you too much, as they're still getting what they paid for, aren't they? Make sure you leave your major sex scene to the final chapter – readers will appreciate you saving the big laughs for the end.

Comedy: This can lighten the direst of situations. It will let your readers know that you aren't really trying for a sequel to Anna Karenina set in Starbucks, even if you thought you were.

Jobs: Always give your heroine a vaguely interesting job, e.g. events manager rather than systems analyst. But nothing so demanding that she isn't able to wonder 24/7 why she's not married to Brad Pitt.

Interior monologue: Your main character should keep a diary (a bit passé – you've obviously heard of Bridget Jones) or a blog (very modern), or else have a friend who gets to hear more daily stream of consciousness than Virginia Woolf's husband.

Chick lit: Under no circumstances should you or your publishers refer to what you write as 'chick lit'. If anyone describes your work as 'light and frothy', always compare it with the difficulty of making a perfect soufflé (even if you've never made one yourself because it's too boring). If totally desperate, you are allowed to compare yourself with Jane Austen, while remembering she rarely included drunken sex with dodgy partners above Clapham launderettes.

Bet You Didn't Know This ... or What You're Assumed to Know by the Age of Forty

- How to unblock drains and toilets.

- The best shops with ego-boosting fake sizes.

- How to give speeches at a moment's notice.

- How to make a citizen's arrest.

- How to lead a political party if ever called upon.

- The company's old mission statements, so that you can all have a laugh.

- The best look when gravitas is called for.

- The computer passwords of everyone in the department.

- What an Act of God is in insurance company policies.

- Whether *Mastermind* questions are getting easier.

- The words of every Christmas anthem written between 1971 and 1990 so that you can lead the karaoke at the Christmas party.

- The birthdays of everyone in the department.

- How to arrange a guinea pig's funeral.

Big Brother

Feel very, very guilty and keep it quiet: you're no longer sure if you really care any more what happens to a bunch of dysfunctional and moronic exhibitionists who like to sit around for hours eating crap food, never doing the washing-up or talking about anything very interesting.

A basic working knowledge of the latest meaningless goings-on in the House can, however, be useful for bonding with teenage children and younger work colleagues: conversationally, it may pre-empt the latter telling you what they will probably be having for their tea. The former may be tempted to finally put you back in the ranks of the 'possibly human after all'. Only don't then let yourself down by saying you don't blame Ken Russell or Germaine Greer for leaving *Celebrity Big Brother* in a huff. This will only give the game away and reveal your true geriatric age.

Big Four-O, The

No one is quite sure why forty and not thirty or fifty is especially significant – nor why people need to remind you of it *ad nauseam*. There's not much you can do about this event – but you can't help wondering why if it's such a big deal, the presents they give you are usually, quite frankly, pathetic. Four long uphill decades on this earth, and for this you're given a cellophane gift box with a barely alive rose to put down your throat and gag.

Many newly forty-fied people feel that if they're going to have to endure the humiliation and embarrassment of this dark night of the soul, they might as well get something out of it. We suggest fortieth birthday gift lists be made available at all major department stores as soon as possible, and that they definitely include gold-tooled DVDs of *Lost in Translation* and nice mirrors that only show fleeting glimpses of the good bits.

Big T-Shirts That No One's Worn Since 1989

At the age of forty you're officially allowed to wear those big T-shirts from your wardrobe without feeling that you're letting yourself down. After all, you're now officially DOTFR (Definitely Off The Fashion Radar) and can wear anything you want, and after all why give them to a charity shop when they look so much better on their original owner – especially when conveniently covering at least half your body?

For maximum effect they must be at least fifteen years old, preferably vibrant and neon enough to cure colour blindness and be saying something Meaningful, ranging from 'Free Nelson Mandela' to your company's mission statement if you feel you really don't care any more.

Biological Clocks

There is only one kind of clock that ticks louder than ever now, with the intention of reminding you of one thing and one thing only: this is your last chance not to spend the next twenty years feeling guilty for serving fish fingers and guaranteeing that what's on the plate is definitely a vegetable-free dead animal.

Do you really want your only legacy to the world to be a

perfect home or would you like it to be decorated with finger painting as soon as possible? While some people will regard your plight sympathetically and let you know that you wouldn't quite be the world's oldest mother, others like to suggest with some malicious glee that it is your fault for leaving having a baby so late and selfishly pursuing your career. All you can do is weigh up the pros and cons and have a quiet word with your mother about whether it was really worth having you. On the other hand, this might not be such a good idea ...

Birthdays

For those who've had children, birthdays – sadly – can never be quite the same again. Whether it's the shopping in Toys Я Us, getting the party theme right or the cost, they tend nowadays unsurprisingly to trigger an allergic reaction of fear and loathing.

And, of course, when it comes to your own birthday, there are now plenty of depressing scenarios revolving around (a) your age – do you really wish to receive 'humorous' cards reminding you that your womb and other internal and external organs are either shrinking or falling to earth? (b) the fact that you've been around so long and have enough gift toiletry sets to sink the QE2. Is there really nothing else they can buy you?

Added to which, the unfortunate truth is that reaching your forties is highly amusing to everyone apart from yourself. You're hardly a spring chicken, but on the other hand still have some miles to go before having people actually respect you. You're definitely on the up and up, but think of it as Shooter's Hill or the highest village in Essex rather than anything for anyone to get very excited about. Eventually, don't worry, you'll get brownie points and hopefully something nice for having survived that long. But in the meantime, some like to remind you that now you've finally passed the point of no return you definitely deserve a present that allows you to draw attention to yourself.

Whether your present is in the form of a day's hang-gliding (we heard you had a death wish), a Ray Mears Survival Day (we heard you liked road kill) or a luxurious spa day (you're a middle-aged woman, goddammit, and we couldn't think what else to get you), they're all felt to be excellent ways of celebrating your mid-life crisis. All you can do is ask yourself, after forty or more years on this planet, do your friends and relatives really see you as a sad, strange person on a suicide mission or in desperate need of deep-pore cleansing?

Favourite Forties Birthday Presents for Men

Buena Vista Social Club
Historical novels about Roman centurion serial killers
Atlas for when the sat nav doesn't work
Nose and ear hair-clippers
Weekend washbag
Greatest Ever Football Matches DVD
Car cleaning kit
Edinburgh Military Tattoo CD
Set of Romanian spanners
Golf ball soaps
Model vintage car
Socks with clocks on
Miniature golf set

Favourite Forties Birthday Presents for Women

Duran Duran's Greatest Hits CD
Book with inspirational thoughts about the menopause

Aromatherapy starter kit
Joanna Harris novel about owning a chocolate shop in France
Trug set
Hyacinth to keep in your cupboard until next Christmas
M&S perfume
Teaspoon to start your collection
Pomander
Scented drawer liners
Gift toiletry set
Ice cream-making set
Pashmina
Padded coat hangers
Rampant Rabbit vibrator with a chocolate

Bloggers

You'd quite like to know where these people, who at one time admittedly would have been burnt at the stake, actually get the time to write so much on a daily basis and with the kind of personal vituperation that only those who would have joined them really care about? When they also manage to do this in proper sentences and paragraphs you're especially jealous and would like to be taken to their time management course leader straightaway please.

Body Piercing

Just as reason separates us from the animals, so horror at having parts of our body stapled with bits of metal and taking several hours to pass through airport security separates us from youth. If, under any circumstances, you still feel tempted, remind yourself to hang on in there as there's always your first hip replacement to look forward to.

Book Festivals

Look around you at any book festival and you can't help noticing how most people hearing Germaine Greer's pronouncements yet again, hanging on every word of Joanna Trollope or who can't get enough of Sebastian Faulks are over forty and female.

Just as Christmas would collapse without the elderly women who spend the entire year panic-buying glittery fir cones, so the serious adult publishing industry is dependent on people who actually have the time to read books that aren't about talking tank engines, anthropomorphic rabbits or Wayne Rooney. The new rock and roll, the chance of meeting Margaret Drabble in the toilet queue or perhaps more time on your hands than you would care to admit? You may just prefer to draw a pashmina over it.

Book Group, Joining a

Does reading *The Time Traveller's Wife* in a book group while drinking a glass of Chardonnay and saying you like a character because he's nice to animals actually mean you've become middle-aged? Or can you claim that by reading more widely you're actually keeping some of the more distressing aspects of getting older at bay?

Bearing in mind that most men are still 'lip reading' Dan Brown, having spent the previous decade doing the same for John Grisham, it's not surprising that women of your age and older are the main attendees and will probably feel a need to discuss a book that doesn't involve serial killing, paranoic conspiracy theories or public schools for magicians.

If your partner, having watched Channel 4's comedy *The Book Group*, is fearful of your involvement in such a hotbed of illicit passion, point out that in reality the opportunities for anything romantic are sadly limited – unless you've managed to find the only man in the country who likes Rachel Cusk.

Boss, The

Usually refers to the person who sums up all your hopes, dreams and fears and is likely to be either (a) the person whose latest '1,000 Days to Total Global Penetration Plan' worms itself into every second of your life, day and night, mainly because you're doing all the work; or (b) Bruce Springsteen, although more likely to worm itself into the core of other people's beings, especially if you hum 'Born in the USA' all the time and can't resist doing the E-Street shuffle when you think no one is watching.

Botox

Few people will ever admit to having had botox. It is, after all, an admission that forty isn't in fact the new thirty, and that without it you'll end up with the face you deserve without any plea-bargaining possible.

Botox is a mixed blessing for your age group. On the one hand, it can make you look more youthful and give you an exciting new lease of life. On the other, it can give rise to the 'have they, or haven't they?' syndrome, by which people ask you searching questions about Bananarama's second number one hit in order to ascertain your real age.

Because it can be fitted in during lunchbreaks, the chances of being found out are low. Except do remember that no one usually comes back after twenty minutes round the block looking quite so goggle-eyed or perky, short of having had ecstatic sex or a major Lottery win.

Botox isn't plastic surgery, of course, and colleagues will revert to their former selves within weeks or months, just in case you're worried that you're going to have David Gest sitting opposite you for too much longer.

Boyfriend

It's a moot point whether you can still claim to have one at your advanced age. 'Mum's boyfriend' does sound a tad Jacqueline Wilson and girlish, as if you'll always be accompanied by a long list of problems and a live-in social worker. 'Lover' makes it sound sexy, but doesn't properly take into account regular bin emptying. 'My man' only works if you have a deep, husky voice and can lie on a chaise longue all day, while 'in a relationship' sounds rather vague and non-committal, as if not many people know his name, possibly not even you. Maybe better not to call this person anything and to just introduce him as 'the person I have sex with and am shacked up with on a semipermanent irregular basis. I do not have five thousand friends on MySpace', just to get any confusion out of the way right at the start.

Bragg, Billy

For fortysomethings who are still feeling angry about the state of the nation and most things else and wish to sing about it in their own slightly discordant way. First it was the Conservatives and yuppies, now it's New Labour and it does seem to be a bit of a downer, doesn't it, sings Billy, as if life's just one horrid mobius loop. What Bruce Springsteen would sound like if he had to sing about the A13.

Brighton

The *sine qua non* test for every forty person – aka do I think getting a used condom up the wheels of my buggy outside Brighton Arts Club is impossibly glamorous or is it just another nail in the coffin of Western civilisation?

Once you would have loved the artistic *demi-monde* and its

high alcohol and other substances-induced raffishness and decadence. Now you stay in an over-priced boutique hotel, can't help noticing how everything's terribly dirty, wonder how drinking wheat grass is going to change your life and if you ever really needed a felt handbag?

Congratulations, you're over forty. Put it like this, your next step is probably a Jane Austen tour of Bath and a visit to an Edinburgh Woollen Mill Shop. It comes to us all.

C

Camden Market

Not for the likes of you. Ever. All the men over forty look like Howard Marks. Let this be a warning.

Campaigning Mugs

What's left of your once fervent campaigning days can be observed at the back of your kitchen cabinet. Here handle-less and chipped 'Viva Sandinista' and 'Coal Not Dole' mugs vie for space with your best John Lewis china.

You haven't quite got the heart to bin them, but don't like the way they scream out 'why aren't you still out there on the streets protesting in your anorak and with your wholemeal cheese sandwiches rather than moaning like a grumpy old person and worrying about your pension?' All you can do is wonder if right-wing causes have nicer tea cups.

Cardigan

Resist all temptations to see this as a perfectly acceptable Christmas present that you cannot wait to try on. It will only open the floodgates to Old Spice, cashmere car blankets and slippers, and before you know it you will be keeping your *Radio Times* in a hand-tooled leather binder and organising your glove compartment.

Career Plateau

By this stage in your working life, your career trajectory may resemble Belgium, i.e. flat and boring, and no one has anything nice to say about you. You are faced with a number of options:

(a) have a late Gap Year and explain you may be away some time being self-indulgent in the Third World; (b) continue with a normal working week and calculate how many seconds are left until your retirement; (c) ask for training so that your colleagues can see how serious you are about Improving the Internal Communications Vision; (d) seriously look at down-shifting and how you're feeling about making boring wooden toys for children in North London.

Cars

Of course, you're old enough to drive a Volvo, an Audi or a Toyota. Seriously, Jeremy Clarkson isn't suddenly going to arrive at your front door and tell you that your penis is going to drop off if you aren't driving a BMW HZR Hydrogen Record car and playing Driving Anthems That My Wife Won't Allow In The House Over Her Dead Body. It's all in your mind, but at your age feel grateful that at least something is.

Cave, Nick

Goth, indie icon, drug rehabilitee and now family man. It's good to know there's still a fortysomething singer rebelling against global capitalism and the status quo who isn't (a) dead; (b) available only on a 'best of …' compilation from Rhino Records; (c) a cult success in Moldavia.

Forties men like to note worryingly that Nick Cave has kept the same look of tight trousers and a sort of mutant mullet and moustache, and may wonder if they haven't gone into Marks & Spencer Blue Harbour a little prematurely.

CDs

If you only buy them in Waitrose because they don't sell any of those nasty ones where people rub their genitals, you must definitely be over forty.

Celebrities

Well, do you know who Kerry Katona is and, quite honestly, do you really care? You have tried to make an effort (a) in the spirit of ironic post-modernism; (b) because otherwise you may never be able to communicate with anyone under forty ever again. But it's not working terribly well, is it? Ask your eight-year-old who reads *Now* to carefully explain who Jodie Marsh is, and why you should care about her, before it's too late.

Center Parcs

Also known as what am I doing sitting in a glorified cloche in February with my family in part of the country a normal person wouldn't ever want to visit. The answer is it's either this or spending two weeks sitting in a size-restricted room in Tenerife in front of the one Pocoyo DVD you remembered to bring with you.

Usually involves stir crazy days watching your children ride on a toy train 9,000 times and commiserating with other adults also reading damp paperbacks and wondering paranoically why they don't sell the *Guardian*.

Centre of Attention

Remember those days when everyone noticed you and hod carriers stopped in mid-hodding as you swept down the street? Well, alas they are no more. The truth is that you may feel you're slowly being erased by that giant rubber hanging in the sky to a mere simulacrum of your original self. Of course, it's a delicate balance between completely becoming part of the furniture and drawing attention to yourself. You may decide eventually, like most of us, to compromise and just wear what falls out of the wardrobe and hope it doesn't attract too many local labradors.

Childlessness

Being childless in one's forties can make you the target of a wide range of sympathetic and less sympathetic comments. These include:

'They'll never know what it is to have their Dyson permanently blocked by a Play Person.'

'I wonder if they're having sex the right way?'

'I expect they cry every night.'

'It's only fair that she should have her career plan ruined too.'

'They'll never live in a starter home in Chelmsford that's too small for them.'

'Is one of them gay but doesn't want to admit it?'

'Imagine only ever having expensive foreign holidays and white designer clothes.'

'Christmas must be a lonely and desperate time.'

'I don't think being a wonderful uncle quite lets him off the hook. We all know who gets left with the dead pets and the serious vomit.'

'I think loft living and just sitting on big sofas doing nothing and thinking you've got a lifestyle is a bit embarrassing after thirty-five.'

'Just imagine, their own parents will never know the joys of desperate emergency childcare.'

Tina and Trevor, the childless fortysomethings

Their friends are jealous and sad for Tina and Trevor in about equal amounts (although this does vary with how much emergency childcare Tina and Trevor are currently lumbered with and whether the under fives have beaten their own incontinence record).

They thought it was accepted that if you couldn't have children, you put all your love and affection into animals (although not rabbits named after members of Westlife who you were convincing yourself would be useful to introduce the children to the death concept, sooner rather than later). But Tina and Trevor hadn't even sublimated their loss by having lots of furry things.

Quite frankly, it was possible to take this as an indirect criticism of those blessed with greater fecundity. Were they really saying disrespectfully 'we're perfectly happy not having any children even though we know our biological clocks are ticking away like nobody's business?' Or were they, to put a finer point on it, having problems in the sex department? And what about their old age without children to ring them up from Australia and ask if they were alright? Their friends wanted to know the truth.

At least, it was generally agreed, Tina and Trevor had attempted to fill this big gap in their lives by offering very generous childcare assistance. Everyone accepted this was the least that they could do. It was only right that they had volunteered as angelic aunties and avuncular uncles, godparents, unpaid care assistants, nursery nurses, trick and treat co-ordinators, voluntary nativity costume makers and children's entertainers. Their friends didn't see why they themselves should have all the fun, after all. Given the long hours culture and the preponderance of female primary school teachers, they supposed it was nice that their children saw a male role model (Trevor) as often as possible and a woman who wasn't permanently harried and wearing horrid track suit bottoms (i.e. every woman they knew except Tina).

They didn't like talking about people being selfish. They hated using that word and felt awful about it ever having passed their lips. But sometimes they just didn't see why Tina and Trevor should be acting as spooky doppelgangers for their own wished-for lives that seemed to have veered off into a strange no man's land of sleep deprivation and eating up other people's leftover Dinosaur Feet and nasty cereals. And they couldn't help noticing how youthful and unblemished the childless always seemed to look, how figures had been kept, opportunities grabbed, careers remained intact.

There was something strange, even alien, about this fortysomething couple that hadn't ever had Walt Disney's *The Sleeping Beauty* on their car stereo for eight consecutive years. They hadn't even shown any inclination to adopt. Which was just as well, considering the twenty-two under sixteens they were currently responsible for as voluntary carers. It gave them a nice taste of what they were missing. Their friends just hoped they didn't feel too jealous. Except they knew there was a cry for help going on there. Somewhere. There had to be, please.

Children

Deciding to have a child in your forties will always bring out malevolent glee in all the self-appointed child experts in your midst. These feel it's about time you joined the real world of never having a proper night's sleep ever again, and they hope your expensive new handbag is child-urine resistant and has a compartment for unknown sticky substances. Nice, eh?

Chinese Herbal Remedy Shop

You know you're in your forties when you get excited because there's one of the disgusting complaints advertised in the window that you don't actually have – even if it's only blackheads.

Chintz

Is the chintz lamp an ironic design statement from Conran, or are you secretly turning into your parents? Keep it ambiguous, keep it very ambiguous.

Clarkson, Jeremy

Patron saint for all those fortysomething men who feel grossly outnumbered and persecuted by (a) cyclists; (b) pedestrians; (c) drivers of Toyotas; (d) speed cameras; (e) those who make unflattering comments about tight jeans on men over forty.

No one else has articulated the male mid-life crisis with such wit and confidence in its need to turn every journey into an open Utah salt pan test run with Bob Seger's *Night Moves* as road anthem of choice. Those close to you are usually loath to say anything, however, in case you go and attack their family runabout or something.

Clash, The

Everyone breathes a sigh of relief when these are mentioned, as they make the eighties seem slightly less embarrassing in retrospect. Legendary neo-punk group that can still cause middle-aged men to grow misty-eyed and lachrymose and to talk about 'raw authenticity' and 'edge' and generally to make others feel terrible because they only liked Bucks Fizz at the time.

Classical Music

Even those with no interest in classical music and with no favourite pieces suddenly worry that, at their own funeral, it will be assumed they won't mind James Blunt's 'Goodbye My Lover' or Whitney Houston's 'I Will Always Love You' being played.

There's the vague feeling that you may be missing out on something Important, Life Affirming and Profound, and classical music is one of those things that you do when you're a grown-up person and have had every upgrade on your Play-station that's humanly possible. This is why The Greatest Classical Hits Ever Volume 9 CD can now be a suitable birthday and Christmas present even for those who previously couldn't see themselves ever clambering out of the mosh pit. It's called *carpe diem*.

Classic FM

It's easy to caricature Classic FM as being superficial and only ever playing the first three minutes of about ten tunes, interspersed with ads for Saga Insurance. But for the fortysomething it's like going into a special gated community, where everything has been screened for the atonal, discordant, noisy and not nicely symphonic. Only worry if you start whistling Samuel Barber's *Adagio for Strings* and finding yourself breaking down at inappropriate moments of the day.

Clubbing

Are you ever too old for clubbing? It's felt by some that there's no earthly reason why they shouldn't continue with this well into their fifth decade. Clubs after all are usually dark, and under masks of sweat and flashing lights everyone looks as if they have psychedelic chickenpox anyway and they are one of the few places where having poor hearing may actually be an advantage.

Cohen, Leonard

Many people in their forties find themselves getting quite melancholic and meaningful when playing 'Bird on a Wire' (you'd rather not talk about it), 'Chelsea Hotel' (not suitable for children and therefore definitely glamorous) and 'Suzanne' (why didn't any of your girlfriends do interesting things like eat oranges beside the water?). At least your partner now knows the danger signs and is able to leave the room before you give a new meaning to the definition of lugubrious and put on Greatest Hits (*sic*) Volume Two.

Comfort Zone

When you find it, please let us know.

Compliments

As we get older we learn not to fish for compliments as we soon realise that they're frequently not what we wish to hear. While every cloud might have a silver lining, every compliment now seems to come attached with a rather heavy lead balloon:

'You could pass for forty-five' (You are forty)

'I nearly mistook you for someone else' (You're looking completely unrecognisable, are you alright?)

'You look well' (Glad to see you're still breathing)

'You look great' (Er, for someone your age)

'I love the way you're interested in everything' (It's nice that you're still reading a newspaper)

'You're very energetic' (You're obviously on HRT)

'You haven't had any work done, have you?' (No, I didn't think so)

'You know so much' (I don't know why, I kind of assumed you would have early Alzheimer's and be frantically doing Word Searches)

'You look just like your father' (i.e. you could virtually be twins)

Conservative

We may be the most youthful forties generation yet but, try as we might, we can't help but get more conservative. It's a long and winding road to seeing the pros and cons in more things than we expected when we were sixteen. But please don't think you're turning completely into your parents – there's plenty of time for that.

	Your parents	**You**
The Royal Family	Can't get enough ermine.	Don't really like the idea of celebrating Gordon Brown's birthday and someone's got to open bus stations, bless.
Suburbia	Like the idea of everyone living in identical boxes and having neat and tidy lawns.	Quite like the idea of not having an illegal pirate radio station specialising in thrash metal the other side of your chipboard divide.
Etiquette	Everyone saying 'please' and 'thank you' *ad nauseam*.	Getting very excited when a shop assistant says it just once.
Sex	Er, pass.	Seven times a night, of course, but also seeing it as an excuse for an extra lie down.
Clothes	Thinking children should be dressed like members of the Famous Five.	Er, Johnny Boden.

Footwear   Sensible footwear.   Wearing Clarks shoes as long as there aren't too many animal tracks on the soles.

Consultants

It's only when you get to forty and moan about the office that people look at you with a mixture of impatience and envy and say 'it's a no-brainer: you could always become a consultant'. It's only now that you will be felt to have sufficient bullshitting skills and maturity – a Prada suit is after all wasted on a 23-year-old – to be able to walk the consultant talk.

Few younger people ever say 'hey, I've always wanted to be a consultant, I can't wait to say "this workforce should be decimated" using feelgood corporate jargon'. But, come our fifth decade, we are more likely to make the life-changing decision that we quite like the idea of performing endless scoping exercises, saying SWOT a lot and being able to exit before everyone discovers that what we're suggesting is what they've been saying for years in the office kitchen for free except no one ever bothered to listen to them.

Remember: you will have spent twenty years in meetings being bored and paid a pittance and doodling pictures of women with bubble perms on blotters – it's only fair that you get your revenge.

Cool

At your age you are only allowed to say this with reference to the weather or the temperature of your fridge. Nothing else.

Cup of Tea

It comes to us all. One day you think you're a hard-drinking, hard-living, close-to-the-edge operator, the next you're wondering what that existential void in your life is and then realise it's a gap that can only be filled by having not just a cup of tea, but a nice cup of tea.

Wherever we are and whatever we're doing, this spectre now haunts us, demanding satisfaction at the sight of the smallest gushing teapot. Nothing else can be done until we've had that adrenaline non-rush. It may sound sad and make us feel like some shocking gallon-drinking harridan off *Coronation Street*, but it's nice to know how easily pleased we are. There we were thinking we had complex 21st-century needs when, lo and behold, a cup of Twining's Best English Breakfast and the right biscuit turns us into Mr and Mrs Mellow Laid Back at the drop of a teaspoon.

Does this mean, then, that fortysomething anxiety and fear and loathing is much overrated? We'll just have to have a nice cup of tea – not in a polystyrene cup and only a little milk thank you very much – to think about it.

Cut Price CDs

At first you can't believe your luck when you see that all your favourite groups and singers from the seventies and eighties are drastically reduced. But then grow depressed when you realise that no one else in the industrialised world wants to listen to songs from the Dr Strangely Strange back catalogue any more apart from you.

CVs

By the time you're forty, your CV will resemble a cross between a ten-part historical epic and one of those experimental novels that doesn't make much sense. It's not surprising really because, with over twenty years of working, you've amassed a range of skills and qualifications that are seriously out of date.

Seeing younger colleagues assiduously working on their CV reminds you that you may have rather neglected yours. Do you really wish people to know that your number one IT skill is designing birthday cards with Regency Lady clip art? Is moon walking still a viable 'key skill'? And do you omit your date of birth which automatically says 'I am older than you think but let's keep it guessing until the interview when you can ask me humiliatingly about it'?

It makes it even more urgent that you do some rapid updating and at least let everyone know that you're not a desperate fortysomething but, er, only semi-desperate.

The Desperate Fortysomething's Updated CV Guide

You say	You mean
Extensive range of transferable skills.	Ten years spent looking after children and spelling your name phonetically to bank staff.
Experienced in Change Management.	Given a P45 enough times.
Long-range thinker.	Last training course I attended was when colleagues clapped because I managed to send a fax.
A player.	Mainly 'Minesweeper' *circa* 1988.

Strategic thinker.

Got so used to being made redundant that I seriously considered setting up a business providing Extra Big Man Size tissues for all those out-placement sessions.

Life coaching skills.

Frequently give younger colleagues the benefit of my long experience at the company, i.e. tell them to get out at the earliest possible opportunity.

Youthful attitude.

Obviously over forty.

Photograph attached.

Oh dear, must have fallen off.

D

Dad-dancing

No one is quite sure what leads to dad-dancing in the mature male. A number of theories have been propounded, including the Feel The Fear And Do It Anyway one, i.e. he never had any idea of how to dance in the first place, but has even less now and thinks that thrashing and un-coordinated limbs will eventually produce something that may actually be called a dance movement. The evidence for success is thin on the ground – but he's well past caring anyway.

It will have struck the observer that the dad-dancer prefers to produce the same identical movements whatever the song. This is because, to him, there is no known distinction between, say, hip hop and a Strauss waltz. It is merely an opportunity for him to gyrate as best he can with a strange look on his face as if he is being slowly electrocuted.

He is usually accompanied by cries of 'what on earth is he doing?' and 'if he's on something illegal can you make sure I don't get any of it?', but has plenty of space around him as no one is quite sure what he'll do next. He would ideally, of course, prefer the piece of music to always be 'Alright Now' or 'Come On Eileen'. But even he knows this cannot always be accommodated.

It's important to note that no amount of discreet or indiscreet choric commentary will make any difference. The dad-dancer is both born and made and the strange primeval flailings that can be triggered by any semi-darkened room and a few coloured light bulbs will always sadly return even after he's been given a strict talking-to by his children.

A cry for help? A triumphant return to an elemental mosh pit? Some kind of basic communication is undoubtedly taking place, it's just that no one is quite sure with whom. Medical attention is rarely needed and the dad-dancer will just need to be left alone by himself until the condition has passed or someone plays Eminem's 'Just Don't Give a Fuck', at which even he must sadly admit defeat. Failing this, partners – in a condition of terminal embarrassment – will whisper the magic words 'Thin Lizzy's Greatest Hits' into his ear as a last desperate attempt to at least get him to go and do it in the privacy of his own bedroom.

Daily Mail

We may not be of that paper's political persuasion or feel quite as grumpy, but there will be times when we find ourselves secretly agreeing that teaching all the Kings and Queens of England is the only way to deal with the ASBO problem. It comes to us all, but it's a good idea to resist telling off children in the street who aren't ours until we're wearing our first suede elbow patches.

Damart

A sizzling love affair that you know could sadly run and run, and definitely one of the best-kept forty secrets.

We know that making it sound all modern and fashionable – with no mention of staying thermally heated or looking like a boiler padded with pink lagging – is supposed to make you feel you haven't quite become your mother or grandmother yet. But at least you realise who is kidding whom. Having spent all those years wondering who ever goes into a Damart shop, you now know the answer: you.

It's just a shame no one else sees you wearing Damart apart from your partner, who knows he's required to make flattering comments about your fluffy thermal Arctic body warmer and not ask if you're ever going to take it off indoors. Remember, they can't take this away from you – certainly not without a long and uphill struggle with the best of the British Spandex industry.

Dangerous Book for Boys, The

Ideal gift for any forties man who might be having doubts about his masculinity and feels that learning about how to tie a reef knot and catch minnows might possibly help.

Dating

Many fortysomethings will have last dated seriously around twenty years ago. This was a time when Wham were number one and *Dynasty* and padded shoulders still ruled, and obviously this could leave some people thinking that wearing a day-glo ra-ra skirt and humming 'Wake Me Up Before You Go Go' are all that you still need to meet a suitable partner. For those who may need to get a little more real, we offer a beginner's guide to modern dating:

Speed dating: Instead of just one person saying they're going to the toilet and then exiting without paying for their drinks or saying goodbye, you'll now have ten, you lucky thing.

Internet dating: At least it means when you actually meet someone, neither of you has any embarrassing things left to say, as they've probably been covered in sufficient depth already.

Friends Reunited: If you really think the person in your class you never wanted to see again and who's been stalking you on-line for the past five years is now the person of your dreams, it's up to you.

Office romances: Due to the long hours culture, we're now more likely to have affairs with our colleagues. This isn't very surprising when the only other people most of us see during our 24/7 week clean our desks or work in late night garages.

Sexual etiquette: It's now more common to take off your leg warmers.

Same sex: You are now no longer required to wear leather shorts, look like someone out of the Village People and have a big bunch of keys, especially if you're not currently the office janitor.

Divorced and Loving It

For women in their forties, getting divorced now apparently worries them less than their children's education, work and the menopause. For men it means yet another mid-life crisis, claiming that no one understands them and buying a re-issued Simple Minds CD, because at least someone somewhere felt their pain in 1981.

Dogs

Remember these don't have to be a sign of middle age unless you start claiming that (a) no one listens to you apart from your dog; (b) no one talks to you apart from your dog; (c) no one can be your friend who doesn't like your dog licking their face and having sexual intercourse with various parts of their anatomy because 'he really seems to like you'.

Downshifting

It's not a decision you'll want to take lightly, but as you reach the mid-point of your life you may begin to question where it's going. Do you really want to attend another six hour stationery requisition meeting? Are there hidden talents you want to develop that you'll otherwise regret for the rest of your life? Do you now have actual proof that your boss is a Klingon?

The first step will be to ensure that you and your partner know exactly what to expect and ensure she doesn't just try to palm you off with running a Boy Scout pack or a Ray Mears Adventure Weekend near Dartford. It's usually men, by the way, who want to downshift. This may not surprise many women.

You: I thought it would be good for us to talk.

Her: I agree. And I've had a think about what you said.

You: I'm so glad, darling.

Her: You could have another shed.

You: Darling, that's not downshifting. I don't think you understand.

Her: Oh, I suppose we're going to be living in a sustainable tepee made out of goat's skin and willow branches and using a compost toilet in the middle of nowhere?

You: How did you guess? But it's not in the middle of nowhere. It's in the middle of a wood.

Her: And how do we survive exactly?

You: I thought we could make organic fertiliser bricks on the back of what we collect in the compost toilet. In lots of buckets. Apparently it's 100 per cent organic. Of course, it would take time to get it off the ground. I was thinking initially we could diversify and see what we could do with Joey …

Her: The dog?

You: I thought you could weave the dog's hair. A spaniel's hair is a bit wasted when you think about it and it would be very sustainable.

Her: So I spend all my time setting back the cause of feminism by about 800 years?

You: Not all your time, because there would be the children's home education to consider.

Her: Home education?

You: It would be too far to send them to the nearest school.

Her: And you think the children are going to agree with this?

You: I just think we need to make it sound attractive. Let them know what fun there's going to be. It would bring us closer together as a family. At least in a tepee in the middle of the woods ....

Her: No one would hear us scream.

You: What are you doing with that sample organic fertiliser briquette, darling?

Drinking

In your twenties, heavy drinking is felt to be impossibly glamorous and desirable and an excellent way of socialising with friends. By forty, however, you will be felt to have 'problems' unless you are a legendary rock star, preferably not quite dead, like Shane MacGowan of The Pogues, who many fortysomething men like to feel is drinking for them personally, especially on Christmas Day for some reason.

Duran Duran

It's easy to smirk at your mother's obsession for all things Cliff Richard, but have you ever thought that your on-going fascination with Simon le Bon and the boys isn't really all that different? When is iconic iconic and when is it just four not quite fat blokes in white suits and red bandanas who aren't stupid and have suddenly realised that you're a demographic timebomb?

Dylan, Bob

Even if you've avoided him all your life, you're now expected to make a big attempt to understand why everything he sings is deeply meaningful and to feel excited that he's still being obscure after forty years. Always call him Dylan, by the way, and have a strange astigmatic look every time he's mentioned if you want to be taken seriously. If you're not reading *Mojo*, you soon will be.

E

Eccentric

Congratulations, your new found decade is probably the first one where you can be truly yourself. While your younger self was only confident enough to reveal limited personality traits so as not to put off prospective employers or partners too much, your forties gives you a clear run. Think of your earlier life as a mere practice slope for bizarre and grotesque behaviour before the final downhill slide.

After all, as you now say to yourself, you only have one life and why shouldn't you wear your comfortable big pants on a more regular basis? The cruellest around you might like to say that it doesn't really matter any more, but don't listen to them as they're only jealous. We still live in a dull, conformist age and need people like you to bring a little colour into our dreary monochrome lives. Just think of yourself as one of the wilder colours of the spectrum, usually only now seen in Early Learning Centres and tell your boring inner chartered accountant what to do.

In your younger days you were probably hideously tied by fashion. But all those unwritten rules and regulations can be completely banished to the back of your wardrobe. In fact, just open your packed wardrobe – you could have a good twenty years of assorted clothes and it's now up to you to wear them just the way you want, like a one-person e-Bay. Why not be your own fashion designer too, as you simultaneously pile on, in no particular order, assorted garments from your previous two or even three decades in the vintage and retro style statement of the year. It's your look and no one can take it away from you.

They might be the sort of clothes that brought M&S to the

brink of financial ruin or the kind last seen bulking up landfill sites in Essex. But mix and match, mix and mismatch – who cares, as like a butterfly out of a pupa you emerge, and Millets meets the 1987 Kay's catalogue. No one can tell if you're about to take the dog for a walk or are going for an all-night disco. Remember, you don't want to hide your light under a bushel, but under a fleece deer-stalker.

But, of course, this is only the start. Eccentrics didn't get where they are today by just looking the part. They've also got to act and speak it. In your case that means, now that you've hit the Big Four-O, never again having to say or do what everybody else is doing just for the sake of boring social convention.

That's why you'll find yourself becoming even more outspoken in shops ('I know you have an allergy to Her Majesty's Coinage, but I only need your attention for a minute'). At work you'll want to let everybody know what you think in a meeting ('Er, twenty people take three hours to decide the purpose of a meeting is to communicate?'), while being equally assertive in the bank ('I'm sure you are – and I'm even more sorry, I've had to wait twenty-five minutes') and naturally in bed ('Duh, not like that!').

Some people will find your eccentricities amusing, while others may take a little time to get used to them. Don't listen to your detractors – how dare they say that like Janis Joplin's freedom it's just another word for nothing left to lose. Only you know if you wish to keep your eccentricities mild, strong or even-Salvador-Dali-wouldn't-have-done-that. Remember, there still aren't enough truly eccentric people in our society. Everyone's relying on you and if you're not singing the 'Funky Chicken' song to yourself complete with clucking effects in public places, you're going to be letting an awful lot of people down, including yourself.

Edge

Of course, a younger you liked music, films, plays and books that were 'darkly edgy', 'nervy and electrifying' and 'a walk on the wild side'. But now that you can get enough of this at home any evening of the week you don't see why you should have to pay for it.

Eeyore

Is probably forty, seeing that his stuffing is falling out, he's terminally depressed and surrounded by annoying energetic younger things who know that the only way to cheer him up is to give him a nice jam jar with a burst balloon for his birthday, about which he is expected to be sadly euphoric.

E4

Best to listen to Russell Brand on Radio 2 in case you feel embarrassed about not wearing a tight T-shirt or having a pink enough mobile phone.

Eighties

Trust this to be your decade. Have you ever noticed that people talking about other decades are always able to find something positive to say, but when it comes to the eighties there's a heavy silence? It is, admittedly, difficult to find many fans of the decade dominated by the sound of Margaret Thatcher and synthesisers. The sixties, of course, are automatically wonderful and even the seventies, the decade that taste forgot, are now felt to have a certain retro charm – but not, alas, the years that followed. You try not to take it personally, but can't help having a terrible inferiority complex.

But was your Nan an opium-crazed Charleston dancer just because she was young in the twenties? Did your dad become a teddy boy because he came of age in the fifties? Then why should they expect you to have distinct mullet tendencies just because you were young and impressionable and once wore a Jane Fonda sweatband?

You definitely deserve to start feeling a little more positive about the decade that made you what you are. We provide a check list below to help boost those plummeting self-esteem levels:

Before eighties	**Eighties**
Legs were boring colours and often got cold.	Rainbow leg warmers.
Children were bored.	Children were given Rubik Cubes and found themselves sitting in corners of rooms for several years.
Punks getting a little boring as every comedian's target.	Yuppies.
People had to stand around in nasty telephone boxes.	People had convenient four-foot-high mobile phones.
People had tedious typewriters.	People had Amstrad computers and phoned their friends excitedly when the paper came out of the printer.

Etiquette, or Things People in their Forties Really Shouldn't Do

When people in their forties were born, the world was a different place. RAC patrol men saluted drivers, people queued for public transport, there was public transport and children bought savings stamps with pictures of Princess Anne on them.

Etiquette should be a subject increasingly close to your own heart and, let's face it, by now you can do a fierce 'tut tut' with the best of them. But with the difference that you aren't yet quite ready to annihilate everyone off the face of the earth or to ask Lynne Truss to be your own personal Rottweiler. Unlike the older Grumpy Person, you still have to live in society and try to behave as a normal person without everyone avoiding you in Sainsbury's.

What a lot of change you have seen in your life, admittedly, but that seems no excuse for you to completely jettison a lost time of courtesy and acting your age. Of course, no one expects you to start knitting a jumper with an appliquéd picture of Prince Philip just because you've turned forty. And we won't expect you to write to Radio 4 because *You and Yours* is under threat again. Yet it may slowly dawn on you that you should sometimes be setting an example as a mature person, even, gulp, a role model. Of course, you never seriously thought you'd hear yourself using these grown-up words. But you secretly know there are some things even you shouldn't do:

Say fuck a lot
Unless you're Dorothy Parker in a Manhattan bar dishing out your *bon mots* and expletives to all and sundry, it's probably best to save yours for flat pack furniture instructions.

Put their feet on train seats
We know you're supposed to be the new thirty or twenty,

but you're not the new ten. If you really must put your feet on train seats, like everyone else, at least take your shoes off, use a newspaper and look guilt-riddenly apologetic, as if you have a distressing cardio-vascular condition which you can't do anything about. Under no circumstances spoil the effect by wearing an iPod, eating a burger and reading a copy of *Heat* at the same time.

Wear tight jeans

For forties people, below the waist is not an area of the body that you will ever wish to draw attention to again. Think of Jeremy Clarkson or, if this fails to work, Kate Moss's weight, height and body mass versus yours.

Use MySpace

It's extremely creepy to have older people hanging around cyberspace trying to find the essence of their lost youth, not to mention marketers often of a similar age attempting to sell products no one wants. Please let youth have its own chance to experiment and discover its own lifestyle mutations in the privacy of their own extended bedroom.

Be able to text too proficiently

Everyone knows that all you need to be able to tap in is 'When will you be home?' and 'Your dinner is in the dog.'

Start imitating the writers of *Is It Just Me or Is Everything Shit?*

We don't like it either, but some of us have to shop at Ikea, drink in Starbucks and vote for political parties who are the best of a bad bunch and don't want to be made to feel more guilty than we already are, thank you very much.

Speak like our children

That means no irritating sentences that can't stop getting

higher and higher and are in serious danger of floating away. We're not Beverly Hills Princesses who spend all the day buying handbags, goddammit. And never saying 'like' or 'excuse me' or 'whatever' in that particularly irritating way they do, even if you're trying desperately to keep the channels of communication open with your teenage offspring.

Think *Sex and the City/Desperate Housewives* are based on real life
Can we break it to you gently?

Wear goatee beards
Why do you think they made middle-aged David Brent wear one? Enough said.

Wear cargo pants
Because everyone will think you're just very overweight as opposed to just being overweight. And you'll probably forget which of those multiple pockets you put your mobile phone in and when it rings will be seen feeling yourself like a middle-aged gangsta rappa, which is not a good look in Homebase on Saturday mornings.

Have a tattoo
Just no.

Go unshaven
Rarely a good style after forty-five, as you'll start looking what they like to call 'grizzled'. Only alright if you're thinking of frightening away persistent Jehovah's Witnesses, don't mind being mistaken for someone wanted by the police for questioning, or want someone to say 'hey, has anyone ever told you you look like Ernest Hemingway during his suicide period?'

Euphemisms

Everyone in their forties can look forward to being the proud recipient of a brand new range of euphemisms, just in case your family and other people feel a little embarrassed about calling you a sad old git directly to your face.

The fortysomething euphemism guide

Distinguished – Either going bald or grey

Very distinguished – Totally bald or grey

Girlish – Obviously on too much HRT

His/Her own person – Makes Marilyn Manson look conventional

A comfortable dresser – Looks like a bag person

Youthful – Still plays air guitar

Looks so well – Botoxed to the eyeballs

Looks incredibly well – So did Michael Jackson for a short time

Lots of personality – Not much else going for them by this age

Young at heart – Embarrassing person

Mid-youth – Talk about kidding herself: just because she got a plastic clutch bag free with *Red*

Always a calming influence – Usually asleep

Everett, Rupert

Ridiculously handsome and youthful-looking 47-year-old British actor based in Hollywood who has starred with Julia Roberts, Madonna et al. Don't let it depress you too much though: he isn't married and hasn't got any children, so doesn't really count.

Exercise

It suddenly hits you with a vengeance that you're unfit and something has to be done. This is why fortysomethings and health clubs are such a wonderful marriage of convenience: each knows the other's imperfections but are happy to over-look them, blaming either temporary amnesia or big financial incentives.

It's only when you enter the changing rooms for the first time that you realise what they've been keeping from you: you have to take your clothes off in front of total strangers. Fortu-nately everyone is discreetly staring at a fishing programme on Sky and you are allowed to put on your gym kit without embar-rassment. On the other hand, you worry why no one is looking at you. Is the sight of you with no clothes on actually that hideous and disturbing?

Of course, no one wants to worry you too much, which is why the health club loves to emphasise the feelgood side of fortysomething exercise; this includes being frothed-up in the jacuzzi, watching *Murder She Wrote* on the plasma screen as an excuse for a little light exercise-biking, and holding a water bottle at all times in order to suggest that you're having a lifestyle.

Even the personal assessment isn't too insulting, chiefly because no one's actually going to say 'you're so fat and unattractive that we won't be able to allow you to pay our exorbitantly priced direct debits'. Instead they do seem to be suggesting rather a lot of swimming, i.e. at least the water will support your great weight and keep you hidden as much as possible. Not to mention Aqua Aerobics – just in case you've never been part of a human tidal wave before and like wearing a float while frolicking in chlorine to Zorba's Dance.

You wouldn't say the gym itself is a surprise, but as a cross between your worst-ever school sports nightmares and what is never shown at Guantanamo Bay, no one can truthfully say that it is geared to the needs of the averagely unfit forty-year-old. If you thought it was embarrassing stripping in front of total strangers, try adding grunting, heavy breathing, gurning, involuntary dribbling and ten different ways of saying 'I'm going to die' to your bundle of tricks. Soon everyone will know your body as well as your partner does – many would say even more intimately after your unsuccessful pelvic thrust with the Swiss ball. All you can do is remind yourself that you are actually paying for this – voluntarily.

Gym etiquette for fortysomethings

Don't tell a member of staff that you don't appear to have a pulse. They will know you are a first-time fortysomething.

Always start off with the humiliatingly easy warm-up exercises, as it is an ego boost to know that you can at least do something.

But don't embarrass yourself by punching the air and screaming 'y-e-e-s-s' as you assume the warm-up exercises are all you have to do.

Just because you actually know the words to Kylie

Minogue's 'Can't Get You Out Of My Head', there is no need to mime to them while exercising. Leave this to her.

Don't scream out 'I'm feeling the burn!' after two minutes on a glorified rocking horse.

Always keep your private parts covered up in the changing area. There will be a towel big enough, don't worry.

Kate and Jon, the expectant fortysome-things

'Our names are Kate and Jon. We live in East Carshalton, where we've led narrow and selfish professional lives, been on expensive long-haul holidays and, until recently, never gave having a child a moment's thought, as obviously it would affect our lifestyle big time. It was only when I started crying every time we saw a baby that we knew something was wrong, and we had made a big mistake. We now realise we are at fault, but hope that Fate's comeuppance has now helped us see the error of our hedonistic ways and we will be better people as a result.'

Kate didn't actually introduce herself to the ante-natal class like this. But she might as well have done. She felt judged. Because one glance round the hall told Kate that she was the oldest mother-to-be. In fact she was Methuselan in comparison with everyone else. She thought there was one other couple who might know the words of a Joy Division song at a push.

There were other men who might have been as old as Jon. But men didn't really count – they were just one up from artificial inseminators when you thought about it.

It struck Kate, who had had time to do a quick bit of mental arithmetic, that most of the other mothers were twenty years younger than her. Which meant she could have been their own mother in another life (she did another bit of mental arithmetic and realised that she would then be the grandmother to today's unborn babies, but preferred not to go too far down that particular route at that moment).

Kate didn't actually feel old. She was forty-five. The magazines had said it was all perfectly fine as you had a more mature outlook and to remember what Cherie Blair and Gordon Brown had done, though obviously not together.

She admitted she and Jon had left it a little late, but there had been a lot to achieve in her professional life and they'd never have been able to afford their nice home otherwise. It was different for everyone. Except she didn't say any of this to the class. She didn't want to be seen as the difficult one and was trying to be very careful. She knew there were expectations about middle-aged career women like her. They had been in control all their working lives and people thought they didn't want to let go now.

Kate's childless friends had a kind of appalled fascination when she told them she was pregnant. But already she felt as if she was living on a different planet – or did she mean deep under the ocean? She certainly felt as if she was wearing lead boots and had never been so tired.

She heard one of the other women saying that hers

was the result of a split condom. Well, hers wasn't. She wanted this baby. It was her most carefully thought out project yet, and she had had many of them. The only person who spoke to her was the young woman beside her. Her name was Jules. Kate smiled at her and said how excited she must be too. Jules, who was seventeen, said she supposed so. She had two children already. She only came because her social worker said her benefits would be cut if she didn't. Jules sighed wearily and said she didn't know how much longer she could go without a cigarette. She wasn't looking forward to giving birth because they wouldn't let you smoke.

Kate smiled. You couldn't do anything else really. Her name was Kate and for the first time in her life she didn't know what to expect. Not at this particular moment. She was waiting for the Life Force to come back. She knew she could rely on it. It had been fairly reliable up to now.

Experience

While everybody else around you is freaking out and claiming it's the end of the world, at least you'll have the experience of having been there before. If nothing else, experience teaches you that the end of the world is highly over-rated by younger people and that the number five bus will generally still turn up the same time next morning with its same group of glum-looking passengers reading free newspapers. It's this new-found wisdom that gives you a distinct advantage over those less experienced than you, and if the light at the end of the tunnel is only a train coming, at least you know to get excited, especially on your commuter line.

EXPERIENCE

What experience has taught you by the time you hit forty

Calling your partner by somebody else's name at a moment of passion isn't necessarily a disaster – if you're a man, look on it as your first successful act of multi-tasking.

Next door's grass is always greener because they don't have a family, a urinating dog and a barbecue that thinks it's a leaking nuclear reactor.

There's no such thing as a 'tasteful' office Christmas party; no matter how hard you try, there will always be someone who is hiding a pair of flashing reindeer antlers to put on your head.

Buying sensible 'classic' clothes under the age of fifty always makes you look as if you're hoping to be presented to the Queen and obviously think that a pleated kilt will give you a head start.

However much you support your political party, there'll always be somebody who makes you want to leave and support the ideologically opposite one.

Forties male haircutting styles on offer are generally not advertised in photos, but can be discreetly provided if asked for, together with an unofficial counselling service.

East Cheam won't sound so hilariously funny if you have to live there because you were priced out of Crawley New Town.

Another two seventies revivals and you'll probably be dead.

F

Family Holidays

Once your children are older, planning the family holiday is no longer the fascist dictatorship that you knew and loved. It's a delicate and fraught case of endless compromise, negotiation and give-and-take. The give always from you, of course.

It's always best to start from point zero, i.e. however much time you spend carefully selecting a teenage-friendly resort, it will always be wrong. A place famed for its night life with wall-to-wall clubbing? Boring. Disneyland only a few miles away? Boring. Robbie Williams will visit you and sing exclusively from his latest album? Boring. It's probably easier just to select the Mediterranean version of Eastbourne and let them know there's a really nice bedroom for them to be depressed and moody in for two weeks.

They will always inevitably want to bring a friend. Failure on your part to agree to this will always be met with the longest silence since the first and last time you asked them if they'd done their homework. You know when you are beaten, especially as there'll now be an additional adolescent to accuse you of being embarrassing, wearing too tight clothes and to suggest you put a sack on instead.

Once arrived at the resort, you are faced with the dilemma that they won't want to be seen dead with you, but you worry about the dangers of letting two young teenagers loose in a nightlife scene famed for introducing the Sodom to Gomorrah. The friend is apparently allowed to stay up much later than your teenager and to wear outfits that make Girls Aloud look like a group of nuns in an enclosed order, as you carefully weigh up the lack of options and say yes.

They will spend the first day being bored together and searching for the only branch of Next on the sub-continent, while you and your partner spend anxious hours after dark watching the clock and checking texts. You realise you only have thirteen more days like this. Sometimes you wonder if you shouldn't have gone camping in Norfolk after all – at least no one can slam doors if you've only got Velcro flaps.

Feeling Ten

It is always a cause for concern whenever anyone over ten actually says this, usually with a strange glint in their eye. More prevalent in people over forty who feel a need to suggest that their real frolicsome self is buried just below the surface and is simply waiting to burst out. Will usually lead to strange and unpredictable behaviour as they try to decide if a ten-year-old would work in credit control, possess a mortgage and be responsible for five different lunch boxes on a daily basis. Middle-aged men still playing with I-Boxes obviously have a head-start, of course.

Feng Shui

Eastern philosophy reckoned to direct positive energies into your home and help you to abolish mess, usually involving a complicated kit or consultant. Quite honestly, at this stage in your life, you think an East European cleaner is a better bet and works out much cheaper.

Fertility

Everyone knows that rates of fertility now start plummeting for both sexes. The truth of the matter is that wombs now resemble old dried fruits that have been around for too many

Christmases, while it's suggested that the only hope of finding any fertile sperm in our testes might be through sending in Channel 4's Time Team. Doctors try not to giggle and compare our scans to examples of modern Britart. All we can do is keep our fingers crossed and hope that Charles Saatchi might want to do something with them.

Fiction

As we get older we may have less patience with irritating younger fictional characters and start empathising with an earlier generation. We can't think why.

Mrs Bennett: Imagine living with four Paris Hiltons. No wonder she gets a bit irritable at times.

Bridget Jones's parents: Imagine having your turkey curry so cruelly mocked. It sounds delicious to us.

Adrian Mole's mother: For every self-obsessed paranoid fantasist, there has to be one person with some vague connection to reality and clean underwear.

Gregor Samsa's mother: Was turning into a giant beetle just another typical excuse for a young person to lie in bed?

Charles Bovary: Emma was just a little annoying from the start and, after all, he was marrying beneath him – she wasn't even a dental hygienist.

Fifty

One of the reasons people hate being forty is that their next 'Big One' is fifty. To cheer you up, though, others like to remind you that fifty is the new forty. But does this just mean then that you can look forward to going through your forties again a second time round? No wonder you're feeling a little tired and emotional.

Of course, unlike turning forty when no one worries if you'll mind wearing a Naughty Nurse pouch while a female contraceptive is placed on your head, by fifty, everything will have quietened down. They know you'll be well past that kind of thing by then and would just prefer a nice lie-down. You'll now be indisputably middle-aged and celebrations will be lower-key, more muted and elegiac, even funereal. In fact, you'll find no one seems to care very much and all you can expect are tasteful cards that feature gardening implements. At least there's something to look forward to.

Things we suppose we should do by the time we're fifty

- Stop reading *Heat* magazine.

- Stop knowing what's number one.

- Have a philosophy of life that's not based on (a) a song; (b) a self-help book; (c) the *Daily Mail*.

- Swim with dolphins or any other form of marine life that smiles and doesn't have lots of teeth.

- Feel it's a mark of our maturity when colleagues choose to tell us about their vomitous intestinal problems.

- Collapse early on in a marathon sponsored by an unhealthy chocolate bar company.

- Check your pension plan to make sure it's got the right name on it, but fail to read any of the small print because it's too depressing.

- Finally meet the person who religiously leaves a Bettaware catalogue outside your front door every week to explain that you don't want a basting bottle with brush, although it's nothing personal, but then buy several cat bowl sterilising units for the first time in your life because you feel sorry for them.

- Read *The Da Vinci Code* so that you too can dribble on your fellow commuter's shoulder, so engulfed are you expected to be by its compelling storytelling.

- Find out who the Rosicrucians are.

- Worry that you can no longer be a Young Rotarian.

- Learn to use an iPod.

- Drink more water.

- Find out what the difference is between 'classic' and 'iconic' because you feel this might somehow be important.

- See if your teenager's Goth-meets-the-Apocalypse bedroom is regarded as an Act of God or normal wear and tear in your house insurance policy.

- Decide if you exist or not, and whether to reply to the 'long lost friend' who contacted you on Friends Reunited.

- Find out why Lindsay Lohan is famous.

- Watch ITV2 just once to see what you're missing.

- Talk to a Mormon.

- Read *Ulysses* or at least the *York Notes*.

- Try not to take it personally every time a computer screen says 'your password has not been recognised', as this is your fault after all. But failing to recognise your first primary school is not, however, and you may quite rightly attack your pc and blame global monopoly capitalism.

- Still get at least one question right on *University Challenge*, even if it is about Jason Donovan.

- Have a complete explanation for where guinea pigs go to when they die, with only partial reference to Intelligent Design and no fudging about guinea pig trailer parks in heaven.

- Be able to muster a range of small-talk subjects for popular use, while also being aware that the number of days until Christmas is not the most riveting or calming conversational topic for many.

- Know yourself and your own incompetencies, and, through a realisation that there is always someone who can do every-thing better than you, have a seamless way of maintaining your self-esteem.

- Hold a conversation with a child, Bratz doll, parent and kitchen builder simultaneously.

- Keep a pair of pants (wet or otherwise) for your child, part-ner or parents in your handbag without thinking that this is somehow unusual.

- Explain to a Jehovah's Witness on your doorstep that you're a neo-Marxist Darwinianist Buddhist (or else make a mistake and get some strange looks from the Liberal Democrat can-didate).

- Finally decide if you did it your way, if you have no regrets or if it's more a case of *que sera sera* and you don't want to talk about it.

- Say no to the restaurant table next to the toilet.

- Have acquired a good supply of Dorothy Parkerisms for the bad times.

- Say I'm half way through my life and I don't care any more about who bonked whom or didn't do the washing up on *Big Brother*.

- Keep the channels of communication open with teenage children even if it is just to ensure a clean supply of 'I scored high on my drugs test' T-shirts.

- Ask your child how to make and send a jpeg.

- If you're passed over for promotion at work, ask yourself if you really wanted to sit in a meeting room until eight o'clock every evening sharing a single Bounty Bar with eight other people.

- Remember that you don't have to do a Neuro-Linguistic Programming course just to be nice to people.

- Get over office politics – do you really care about someone who thinks you have a nicer bit of cubicle chipboard partitioning than they do?

- Say 'hello' cheerfully to your colleagues on Monday mornings as an example of civilised behaviour because someone has to.

- Cry during the film of Raymond Briggs's *The Snowman* without embarrassment, even if your children are making gagging noises at the same time.

- Finally know the words to one complete Christmas carol before it's too late.

- Feel all is good with the world, even if it isn't always, because it's good to kid yourself sometimes.

- Have a health scare that makes you realise life is too short to make choux pastry.

- Appreciate that just as you aren't clones of your parents, your children aren't clones of you, and if they want to sit on the ground outside Miss Selfridges most of the time that is nothing to do with your DNA, alright?

- Accept that if you go out without an umbrella, it rains.

- Buy a spare set of Xmas fairy lights.

- Experience oneness with the universe.

Fifty Quid Bloke

Aka having a mid-life crisis in public. New demographic of fortysomething and older men who haunt HMVs on Friday afternoons guiltily buying CDs and DVDs and upon whom the UK record industry is now almost sadly single-handedly dependent. With younger people either downloading or buying on-line, Fifty Quid Bloke is now seen as something of a saviour, as he attempts to re-create his youth by purchasing CDs of New Order and Blue Nile and any contemporary groups that let him think it's 1982 again and he still has a hairline. Personally, we blame Nick Hornby.

Films for the Over-forties

For a number of years it seemed that Hollywood films made for anyone over fifteen who'd had sex successfully and wanted a break from binary opposition were virtually non-existent. Of course, many over-forties sat through interminable Harry Potters with their offspring and tried to remember not to sigh during another epic elf scene during *The Lord of the Rings*, but they were just being polite.

It was only fairly recently – shock horror – that a new range of popular films has appeared apparently geared to the hopes, desires and mid-life crises of a generation old enough to remember the original non-vintage seventies. *Lost in Translation* gave us an angst-ridden Bill Murray on a business trip to Tokyo, trying to resist the charms of the much younger Scarlett Johansson and a Roxy Music soundtrack. In *American Beauty*, Kevin Spacey finds himself on the inevitable journey of self-discovery in the American suburbs, while in *Sideways* two friends visit the Californian wine country as those three favourite forties themes – drinking, divorce and depression – find themselves with major starring roles.

These were good films, but few and far between for a burgeoning demographic mourning the long professional death of Woody Allen as a film maker, but which isn't yet ready for *Tea with Mussolini*. Failing brand new films, what over-forties are hoping to see on their screens are re-makes of some of their most popular titles but with themes and subjects more appropriate to their lifestyles.

Suggested remakes include:

Ten More Things I Hate About You: The cast returns ten years later, married and still screaming at each other, but this time it's more realistic and tends to focus on teeth grinding, failing to brush teeth before sex, always leaving the toilet seat up and keeping the insides of a television in the garage.

The Devil Wore Primark: Meryl Streep's glamorous editor has her own Damascus road conversion, realises machine washable, practical and £5.99 is best and makes life easier for every fortysomething for ever more.

Bridget Jones: Well Beyond the Edge of Reason: Bridget now has three children (triplets came along just when she was on the verge of being promoted to senior media executive) and lives in Essex.

Mission Totally Impossible V: Agent Ethan Hunt at forty-eight finally realises it is, indeed, impossible and he can no longer jump from buildings or climb up mountain precipices in search of enemy agents. Instead he makes the decision to set up an extreme sports company in Palm Springs with Bob Hoskins.

Notting Hell II: Julia Roberts and Hugh Grant married with two children realise that the inner city is no place for children, move to a nice village outside Ashford and Julia Roberts joins Weight Watchers and listens to her old Duran Duran records a lot.

Flattening of Hierarchies

Fashionable business philosophy by which most middle management jobs done by people in their forties were meant to vanish in the interests of a lean and mean organisation. Unfortunately this was not to be, as they discovered that there would then be no one left who was capable of knowing the right grammatical use of 'its' or where the office Christmas decorations are kept.

Fleeces

You'll probably own at least ten of these by the time you're forty-five. They come in a variety of rich colours, and once you get over the rather loaded response that 'it looks nice and warm' from someone who wears other sorts of clothes, you'll know there's no looking back.

Whatever the fashionistas say, fleeces are the *vetements de nos jours*. They automatically suggest that you either have lots of interesting leisure time or else are permanently unemployed but like to alternate between being day-glo lime and looking like a Belisha beacon. Elle Macpherson and other currently fleece-less people in their forties don't know what they're missing.

The fleece is naturally chosen for its cheapness and general bagginess, as no one need ever know any more what happens underneath and whether you are fat, thin or have breasts (male or female). Admittedly it makes everyone look permanently hunched and like trainee Michelin Men, and if on the small size it can appear that you're currently disappearing into a fluffy coloured sack. But this is a small price to pay bearing in mind the warmth and practicality. It is, after all, just a simple matter to throw these multi-tasking garments into the washing machine. This happens frequently, bearing in mind the amount of sticky secretions from children and older relatives they frequently attract, not to mention the number of times your labrador may have given birth on it.

Fleeces never wear out and are virtually indestructible, which may account for the large number in every fortysomething's wardrobe. In fact re-marrying fortysomethings may like to consider a 'no more fleece' pre-nuptial agreement to save them endless recycling trips.

On the other hand, wearing a fleece with pride suggests you may have more important things to think about than ephemeral fashion, even if it is just grabbing something for the school run because you haven't had time to dress. And it does possess the extra advantage that your children will be too embarrassed to be seen with you in public ever again. Don't go anywhere without it.

Folding Bikes

If you're a fortysomething man, there's a statistically above-average chance that you like to ride a souped-up child's bike that vanishes down pot holes at worryingly frequent intervals and collapses on people in trains. This will chiefly be admired by other fortysomething men with folding bikes who like to rap about it. One day, no doubt, the significance of all of this will become clearer to us all.

Football, Playing

Everyone knows that, but for an accident of fate, you would have been playing for the Premier League and changed the face of British soccer overnight. But it's now best to accept suffering humbly and continue your present career in your Sunday Super Grout Cleaner League team where you are seen as invaluable, mainly because they are three men short.

Forty and Fabulous

Ridiculous feelgood phrases that forties are encouraged to use about themselves. We know they can't be more realistic and say 'forty and manic', 'forty and flushing' or 'forty and wearing a T-shirt advertising a garden centre', but we sometimes wish they hadn't set the bars quite so high for everyone.

Fortysomething Achievements

It's easy when the going gets tough and everyone seems to be blaming us for the horrible eighties – or for raising rude children – to forget that people in their forties have been responsible for many little-noticed social advances. The next time some smug baby boomer is talking their earlier generation up, let them know how it was yours and yours alone that:

- Encouraged the boom in Kumon tutors, so that no one, including your children, need ever know that you don't understand quadratic equations, the basic laws of physics, or anything about history apart from Henry VIII's wives.

- Made sure that rock festivals provided decent toilets instead of plague pits, so that even your teenage heavy metaller was grateful.

- Brought back Duran Duran from the dead.

- Talked up British seaside resorts as ideal for family holidays (even if it was basically because you couldn't afford to go anywhere else).

- Made camping fashionable – er, ditto.

- Made the editor of *Mojo* appreciate that there was room for yet another feature on Eric Clapton or Neil Young's health problems.

- Created a market for hen lit – why shouldn't people know what happens beyond the post-partum divide.

- Became Yummy Mummies – why should all those corporate time management skills be wasted when you could be raising your child like a Goldman Sachs fast tracker?

- Saved Bagpuss from oblivion.

We rest your case.

Friends, Fewer

As we reach forty, many of us find we have fewer real friends. While at one time we may have had what seemed to be dozens, now we can often count them on one hand, if not one finger.

Friendships seem to suffer from a natural attrition factor over the decades, assisted by partners (don't like your friends), work (no time to see any friends remaining) and family (why do you want to be friends with someone who sounds like a bad circular letter?). In fact, the more we think about it, the more surprised we are that we have any friends left at all. Speed friendship sessions, if anyone thought of arranging them, could be our last remaining hope as we meet our ideal fellow Clash or Belinda Carlisle obsessive over a Chardonnay and recall where we were during the 1985 Live Aid Concert. But only for the session, of course. We're much too busy for anything else.

Friends Reunited

Aka Last Chance Saloon. It is often felt that forty is the key time for renewing old school friendships. Any earlier and the rich patina of nostalgia and memory loss has yet to kick in properly and you're not sure if you really want yet to see people who remember what you looked like as a misshapen Puck wearing a Green Goddess body stocking; any later and there is a good chance no one will recognise each other and feel terribly depressed and apologetic.

In practice, however, it's only when someone you haven't seen for around a quarter of a century contacts you out of the blue that you ask yourself (a) if you were that eager to meet them then why haven't you done so before; and (b) isn't it rather like having a stalker who discovers various unsuitable pieces of information about your past that you've managed to be in successful denial about for all these years and now wishes to Reveal All? Remember: no matter how sophisticated and grown up you may think you are, to someone from the third year class in 1977 your only claim to fame is being the person who wore non-regulation pants to hockey and got a detention.

You: Sorry, I just supposed that we would have a lot more in common.

Them: On paper it looked good. Well, in 1977 we did.

You: I suppose we shared a mutual appreciation of Kenny.

Them: I only did it because it was my fortieth birthday.

You: Me too.

Them: We sounded different on email.

You: Everyone sounds about eleven on email.

Them: Well, it's good to remember old times.

You: If we don't do it now, we never will.

Them: That's right. You've hardly changed.

You: Fewer spots.

Them: Do you remember when Susan Moore set the chemistry lab alight?

You: I think so.

Them: But didn't you used to have ginger hair?

You: I've never had ginger hair.

Them: Wasn't your nickname Duracell then?

You: Sorry?

Them: We called you after the battery because it had an orange stripe around the top.

You: I think you're thinking of … Er, can you think of her name?

Them: Obviously not. That's why I thought it was you.

You: So you've come all this way for nothing.

Them: So have you. Er, shall we just pretend to our families … it's a bit embarrassing otherwise. You could pretend to be ginger and say that you had 'I love Bay City Roller Eric' on your pencil case.

You: I suppose so.

Them: The past is a foreign country.

You: Except it could do with stronger border controls and tighter quotas sometimes …

G

Garage

You will have reached the age where your garage either looks so neat and tidy that you must be expecting a visit from the Queen, or else like the last day of the Glastonbury Festival except with more half-finished flat-pack furniture. Only you know which state of major psychic disturbance you are currently in denial about.

Gardening

There comes a point in every fortysomething's life where the desire to do strange and complicated things with plants and flowers can no longer be resisted.

It's odd that many of us can get through our earlier decades as reluctant gardeners but now fully equipped with trug sets we can't wait to get our hands into some John Innes, no matter how small our garden. A primal urge to bond with nature? A Marie Antoinette moment? A sudden amour for Alan Titchmarsh? It's probably best to retain your mystery, especially if all you wanted was just to have a nice quiet cigarette without anyone noticing.

GPs

According to medical science, yours is an age when any number of annoying symptoms first make an appearance, although at least some of them may be amenable to treatment.

Doctor: So, you're feeling depressed?

You: Some of the time.

Doctor: And you're tired?

You: How did you know?

Doctor: You think you should lose some weight and go for a Spanish-Ranchero look with Regency undertones like Gabrielle in *Desperate Housewives* and some good Marc Jacobs might help too.

You: You guessed?

Doctor: Because it's my job to recognise symptoms like yours. What you're saying is that you don't feel as perky as Bree. Tell me, have you just seen the complete boxed set of *Desperate Housewives*, Volume 2, including the notorious Bree's new life without Rex episode?

You: Yes, doctor.

Doctor: You were by yourself at the time, with no one to tell you that this is just a soap opera middle-class people think is respectable to watch but, if unchecked, can lead to major addiction problems?

You: I'm sorry.

Doctor: We're seeing a lot of this sort of thing at the moment. Fortysomethings who compare themselves with the inhabitants of Wisteria Lane and find their own lives wanting and completely lacking in interesting faux Renaissance marble figurines. There should be a health warning on that programme. There's only one thing that might cure it.

You: There is doctor?

Doctor: The complete six boxed sets of *The Sopranos*, to be taken one episode a day over several months and you must finish the course.

You: You think it will work?

Doctor: It will make you realise your own family and home isn't as dysfunctional and lacking in colour co-ordination as you thought it was, that you actually haven't got any real problems and that you could pull yourself together and think of the developing world for a change.

You: Thank you, doctor.

Doctor: Don't mention it.

Grandparent

Being a fortysomething grandparent usually triggers rapid and not always discreet mental arithmetic calculations in others. But, of course, it's quite possible for someone your age to have grandchildren without necessarily having had your family at an age and with a fertility to rival Vicky Pollard.

The only problem you may have is an identity one, as the stereotype of the grandparent is still all-encompassing in our society. Even if you're not actually three foot six with curly grey hair, a shawl and glasses, you shouldn't be surprised if that's how your grandchild likes to draw you in pictures. But faced with the Holy Trinity of Walt Disney, Clinton Cards and family role models, it's probably easier just to start knitting now and pretend you're Thora Hird …

Green Tea

Cheap fortysomething de-tox and miracle panacea. Looks terrible and tastes awful, but hopefully might make up for excesses of earlier life if drunk in sufficiently nauseating quantities.

Greetings Card Shop

Those evil places that most of those in their forties try to avoid like the plague if they can help it. Put it like this, if it was people in their seventies being depicted as either impotent idiots or boring office drones there would be a national outcry. But as it's only the forties you'd better have a sense of humour and lighten up, or else just have your nervous breakdown and get it over with.

If Grotesque Card Shop is only a microcosm of society, then there's no doubt how the latter sees you. While ages up to yours are usually benignly depicted, come the Big Four-O every available card seems designed to highlight your obvious low self-esteem, decrepitude or pathetic attempts at sexual intercourse. Friends and relatives should certainly have no trouble finding you a card, judging by the bumper-selection always readily available.

Choose from:

Wistful animal vanishing down hole

Horse alone in field

Technicolour sunsets

Elephant's backside

Woman looking under sheet for husband's penis

Floral tribute in deepest sympathy

Remember that any negative reactions will only engender remarks about you needing a humour transplant/being in denial/obviously having a problem 'down there'. Most forty-somethings like to break down now, tell everyone they love them all and use this as an excuse to visit the lavatory and do their breathing exercises, as they still have their Big Four-O presents to look forward to. They may be some time.

Grey, Going

To make you feel better, people will say it makes you look 'patrician' or 'sexy' and you are up there with Richard Gere or Emmylou Harris (although you thought she had gone white, which is slightly worrying). On the other hand, and this is more likely, you can go to the hairdressers where, beneath a decid-edly non-grey wave of orgasmic euphemisms, you can see it washed away as you decide that perhaps your natural hair colour is actually a vibrant conker after all. To say you're not in denial is like saying that President Bush doesn't need to urgently buy his retirement condominium.

Groups You've Never Heard Of

Is it just an international conspiracy to prove you're over forty when you think a group called Fuck Off Machete is another one of your children's nasty little jokes at your expense? You blame the groups themselves – it's their fault for having monikers you've never heard of and you're sure they do it deliberately. If they only knew the distress it can cause fans of Katie Melua's music (OK, the first six tracks you only ever get as far as on the school run) who are starting to feel quite got at.

Grumpy

Believe it or not, you're still much too young to be Seriously Grumpy. But that's not to say you aren't at risk of developing Mildly Grumpy Moments as befits your new-found decade.

A mild moan about global warming or the state of the government is everyone's right. However, being perpetually or serially grumpy is so ageing and usually rather tedious. It's worth asking yourself how often you really tread in dog excreta, will an incorrect greengrocer's apostrophe actually ruin your children's lives, don't we see enough of Germaine Greer anyway, and do you really wish to be declared a public nuisance? And if you're not very careful, soon you won't be able to leave your house unless you have Jenny Eclair with you to say 'fuck' to everyone.

Save any residual grumpiness for your partner. You know they won't mind – they're used to it.

Guilt

There's probably so much going on by this point in your life that it's inevitable you'll feel yourself lacking in some department. But whether it's your partner, children, parents, career, garden, pet, remember you're allowed to spend one minute every hour suffering maximum recriminations about each of these in turn, as they stack up around you like aircraft above Heathrow. However, under no circumstances do you want them all to land at once and ruin your day completely. You'll save that for when you have more time, like your holidays.

Guitar

An empty room. A Gibson guitar. A fortysomething man. A strange plaintive wailing and a strumming that seem to come from a time and a place not of this world. Someone is trying to communicate. What it is, no one is quite sure. Leave him. He will reach the difficult part of 'Stairway to Heaven' and give up. Eventually.

H

H&M

Is it just you, or is this store always extra long so that it takes eons to hide your embarrassment as you fleetingly pass the racks of zero size clothes before arriving where you feel happiest and most secure? This is at the back, where there will always be bigger, less fashionable and reduced items that they prefer to keep in dark corners for customers like you. If your teenage daughter is with you, she will remind you what you used to say to her, about not being so silly and self-conscious as who wants to look at you anyway? You aren't sure whether to be cheered up or even more depressed. But at least you can always help yourself by pretending to buy it for someone else and enquire, in a loud voice at the till, 'can you bring it back if it's too big?'

Hatcher, Teri

Having your pores examined on TV plasma screens and your face closely scrutinised for signs of plastic surgery, with people asking when you last had a good square meal and if you're anorexic – we're now wondering if being a fortysomething media celebrity is as full of international glamour as they first led us to believe.

Having Children in your Forties: Reassuring Things People Like To Say

'I'd make the most of your difficult pregnancy because having the child will be ten times worse.'

'At your age you won't have any energy ever again and I should forget about Mariella Frostrup – she probably has a fleet of nannies and au-pairs …'

'Do you like Pizza Hut?'

'You don't think you'll keep that sofa white, do you?'

'This is the last adult conversation you'll ever have.'

'Having been called your company's best line manager with negotiation skills to kill for isn't going to work with a three-year-old who won't wait for Acas to see if she deserves a rock star Bratz.'

'It will be the last time you'll ever have sex without feeling guilty because you haven't checked if your child is still breathing.'

Hawkshead

If you haven't already succumbed to the delights of the afore-mentioned catalogue, don't worry, you will. For inconsiderable sums of money you can find yourself lost in a world of odd-shaped cagoules, walking socks, bobble hats and seriously prac-tical jumpers, while Kendal Mint Cake is on offer to give you that elusive Chris Bonington moment. Photos of happy and attrac-tive fortysomethings sitting on dry stone walls in fluffy body warmers having thermos Cup-a-Soups only re-awaken primal and bucolic urges until now buried under the weight of family and career. And you can try it all on in the privacy of your own home without the embarrassment of entering Milletts and feel-ing everyone is whispering 'elasticated plastic trousers' to you.

It's easy to convince yourself that (in the words of the copy-writer) these elasticated gaiters are 'timeless' and 'classic', mainly because they have never been in fashion and have prob-ably been seen by nauseated sheep in the Lake District for longer than they care to remember. But do bear in mind that you will only ever wear these clothes in a local recreation ground and everyone will look at you and your partner in matching cerise nylon ponchos and Alpine boots and wonder if you know something about global warming that they don't. You, of course, will tell yourself that this is only the start. Expect to trade up before too long to Land's End and wear stylish Hyannis Port yachting shorts and pasty-like loafers for a visit to Southwold.

Top ten Hawkshead items for fortysomethings

Packable trousers
Alpine gilet
Polar fleece
Alpine boots
Body warmer
Weekender socks
Fleece gaiters
Trek shoes
Nylon poncho
Farmhouse chutney

Health

You have now reached the point beyond which conventional medicine is felt to be in doubt and everything can be put down to your age.

Forty is when people like to make unprompted and worry-ing comments about your health. Being a spluttering wreck who feels on the verge of collapse will elicit the cheery and heartless comment that 'creaking doors last the longest'. A fit and unblemished health record on the other hand will be regarded with a sombre demeanour and multiple tales of those who never visited a doctor in their lives but were suddenly struck down by a terrible illness at just about your age.

With so many contradictory prognoses around, it's not surprising that those in their forties have taken to complementary medicine in a big way. If you think it helps your inner being, it is after all your right to gag on a milk shake harvested from scum on Lake Titicaca that gives you green lips.

Favourite fortysomething wonder drugs

Omega-3: Most fortysomethings believe that if they take one of these a day it will undo the damage of four decades of dissolute living and may stop Gillian McKeith from knocking down their front door and demanding a sample of their stool.

Ginseng: Aka middle-aged ecstasy. If this doesn't keep you up past *The Nine O'Clock News*, quite honestly, nothing will.

St John's Wort: Who would have thought your depression could be cured by something sheep like to eat as an emergency laxative?

Multi-vitamins and minerals: Taking these is rather like imbibing 5,000 proprietary drugs, or doing the Lottery, in the vague hope that the right combination of numbers might somehow come up and solve all your problems.

Rescue Remedies: Apparently consist of marigold petals harvested at full moon and recommended by those forties who like to draw attention to themselves and still haven't got over the Flower Fairies.

Black cohosh: Thinking you'll be able to cope with the menopause using folk remedies that stain your hands permanently black.

Hen Lit

Being told that the most important things in your life are a man and a glass of Chardonnay is insulting even when you're younger, especially when it slowly dawns on you that you're only reading a disguised Mills and Boon set in Fulham except with more blondes. When writers of chick lit hit their thirties and forties, they usually turn to hen lit in a desperate attempt to re-assure their readers there's nothing wrong with eating up their children's regurgitated fish fingers provided no one knows they're non-organic.

Hilton, Paris

If you're not sure if she's serious or not, or what she's actually famous for, don't worry, you're probably over forty.

Hormones

While in your twenties and thirties no one seemed to have any, after forty they appear to rear their ugly heads once again with a vengeance.

It's like being thirteen again because in a weird kind of new behaviourism, everything you do may now be attributed to them, accompanied by knowing looks from all concerned. In case you didn't know it, you are nothing else but your uncontrollable rampant raging hormones, alright? If you ever believed you even had a little bit of free will you may need to do some serious re-thinking.

If Hamlet thought everyone wanted to pluck out the heart of his mystery, he should try being a fortysomething woman who actually dares to be a sentient being, i.e. like most other people. A perfectly just complaint to the family about having to pick up everyone's socks again? A suggestion to a fellow passenger that maybe you don't wish to hear their 200 Greatest Thrash Metal iPod selection just at the moment? 'It's obviously her hormones', they'll mutter, and all you can do is scream that it's not, which just goes and confirms it for them. Male hormonal changes incidentally result in increased lassitude and general droopiness, about which many woman will only reply 'so what's new?'

Hornby, Nick

Thanks to author Nick Hornby, no middle-aged man need ever be embarrassed again about liking football in a way that would embarrass an eight-year-old, buying an abnormal number of CDs, and wearing a modern version of the blouson and a baseball cap if he really must.

With books like *High Fidelity* and *About a Boy*, the author has explored a new demographic that allows a man to be aware of his more sensitive side and if anyone complains that he is being puerile, childish and irritating he is able to say that he is simply being part of the zeitgeist. These books are also read by women and should, if nothing else, at least let them know what they've got to look forward to.

House Prices

People under forty look at you enviously whenever these are mentioned. You're not quite sure why.

Human Resources

You've been around so long you can remember when these were called Personnel and a nice person asked about your hobbies during the interview and, if you were successful, showed you where the toilet was. You don't think it's so nice today, though, when they give you a copy of the mission statement

and interrogate you about your learning outcomes and everyone looks at you strangely when you mention your CSE in
Proper Cooking and how *Howards' Way* was a seminal influence
on your life.

1

Iconic

By this age everyone's supposed to be concentrating on iconic with a vengeance. A rapid filtering process is going on, by which you only want the best in music, food, cars, art, garden decking – you name it. It's what used to be called 'classic', but the marketers know that at your age you can see through that one – they've come up with something extra aspirational-sounding to make you feel even more like pigs' slops if you don't have it.

Illegal Substances

If you're a typical fortysomething you'll like to think of yourself as a fairly laid back, liberal-minded individual. You may even as a younger person have experimented with certain substances, which may, or may not, have continued, albeit in a discreet sort of way and only at dinner parties. But when it comes to your children, even the most libertarian parent suddenly finds right-wing and repressive hackles rising at the merest mention of drugs. It's why conversations with our teenage offspring are always minefields:

Teenager: Dad, have you ever read Howard Marks?

You: Er, no.

Teenager: You must have heard of him though.

You: Er, yes.

Teenager: He's written this book, *Mr Nice*, about how he thinks smoking marijuana isn't hurting anyone and should be legal. I want to use it for my GCSE coursework.

You: You do?

Teenager: And I thought I could use you as a resource. Did you know that cigarettes and alcohol are supposed to be much worse for you? Dad, did you take drugs when you were at university?

You: I don't know where you got that idea from.

Teenager: Mum said you had a T-shirt that said 'Legalise cannabis' and you had all Bob Marley's records.

You: What about the Second World War? You could do lots of fascinating things about the Nazis. Your grandmother is always very interesting about making a Christmas dinner out of egg powder.

Teenager: Is 'Lucy in the Sky with Diamonds' really about LSD?

You: I don't know what you're talking about.

Teenager: Mum said you wouldn't …

You: She did?

Teenager: … If I promised not to show anyone that photo of you naked and covered in mud in the bad trip tent at Glastonbury in 1983.

You: It must be someone else.

Teenager: It's got your name on the Gandalf hat. I'm going to call it 'The Drugs Don't Work'. Dad, why are you crying on the floor doing funny things with the carpet in your mouth? Does that mean I can use your T-shirt then?

You: Ask your mother.

Teenager: I have. She's ironed it already …

Inner Adult

We're part of the generation that put the permissive into society and that's been taught to want everything now. But we're also adults, parents, employees and responsible members of society. How do we square the two? The answer is, of course, that we don't.

What we do have instead is a constant dialogue between our sensible inner adult and the untrammelled child/narcissist/hedonist that won't take no for an answer. Our inner grown-up has a voice that's a cross between an irritating life coach and one of those even more irritating but sensible British Rail pre-recorded safety announcements. We know what they're saying makes sense, but would prefer to ignore them at our peril. There's a vast range of situations where these conversations are never-ending and we just know this one will run and run.

Mid-life crisis

Inner Adult: You don't think buying a brand new Harley Davidson is a rather obvious way of saying 'I'm having a major mid-life crisis'?

You: I thought it was better than buying a 4 x 4 and saying 'I'm contributing to the environmental crisis.' I think David Cameron should be rather proud of me.

Drinking too much

Inner Adult: It's never sensible at your age to drink too much. Unlike twenty-year-olds, it takes you much longer to recover from the night before.

You: Well, I'm drinking much more slowly than I used to and this must be medically better, it stands to reason.

Pension

Inner Adult: You do realise you should be saving a greater proportion of your income now if you have any hope of a decently funded old age?

You: I'm hoping to sell my old Syd Barrett LPs on e-Bay, alright. One of them was signed by his next-door neighbour.

Top Shop

Inner Adult: You don't seriously think a range of clothes designed for size zero teenage models will fit you?

You: I can wear my daughter's smock as a pashmina for one arm.

Fifty Quid Bloke in HMV

Inner Adult: Don't you think it's a bit profligate spending this amount of money every week on CDs and DVDs you don't really need?

You: I don't know how you can say this about Van der Graaf Generator's unfairly ignored second album now available in a triple gate folded de-luxe imported edition.

Office Christmas Party

Inner Adult: Is it sensible at your age to stand next to the photocopier wearing a Donna Summer disco glitter wig, and without any trousers, when you know someone is going to try and photocopy your genitals?

You: I tried to join the group discussing conditions on the M25 but they crowded me out, honest.

Being childless

Inner Adult: Doesn't it worry you that still partying and leaving having children until your mid-forties is much too late?

You: No. At least I'll be able to discuss the Scissor Sisters with them.

Middle England
Inner Adult: Isn't it about time you settled down in a green and leafy place and expected everyone to listen to you as the representative voice of Britain?

You: I'd rather just watch *Grumpy Old Men* and *Women* and thank God I'm not a ranting loony yet, if that's alright with you.

Work
Inner Adult: You should have a career action plan and work at your CV on a regular basis.

You: I did recently dress my Beanie Baby in Armani with matching briefcase. I think that was a good start, don't you?

Parenting advice
Inner Adult: Listen to Supernanny and you might get some good tips. It looks like you could do with them.

You: I know that whatever I'm doing I'm probably doing it all wrong, but at least I'll only have one person to blame, OK?

Irony

As we get older, irony comes more and more into play. Let's face it, it has to, because otherwise we'd just roll ourselves into a small ball and fall down the back of the sofa like most things in our home. Here are just a few of every forties' favourite ironical things:

- Hamsters will always die on Christmas Day.

- Children always know if dead goldfish are replaced with identical ones, even if they all look the same to you.

- Statistically there will always be one year when you'll have three Nativities and two Xmas Fayres on the same evening and someone will drop a bottle of milk on the kitchen floor one minute after you finally get home.

- If you're a woman, it's not that you don't have plenty of hormones, they just seem to be the wrong type.

- Now that seventies style and fashion is all the rage again, you reckon that makes about half your life to date dominated by those hideous chunky vases and lampshades and nauseating oranges and chocolate browns.

- Just when you've given away about two tons of plastic baby toys and assorted clothes, you'll discover you're pregnant again.

- Companies like to make you redundant on Christmas Eve in order to make it more seasonal.

Is It Just Me or Is Everything Shit?

Young grumpies, old grumpies … isn't there anyone out there any more who has a good word to say for anything? Sorry, that means you're the last white hope and everyone's relying on you to keep the whole show on the road and to be a positive role model for your children and the next generation. No, you're feeling knackered.

J

Jeans

Everyone can remember the days when jeans were the new gold standard, and you and your friends would giggle for hours about someone who wasn't wearing the right Levi 501s. This is very different to today, when you basically have two pairs: the ones you wear for any household task and that feature some interesting bleaching (unintended) and the slightly newer ones you wear for anything else, although you can't help wondering if anyone notices – apart from your children, that is, who don't count and for whom the wrong rip is like social death.

Slim leg, skinny leg, boot cut, cropped? Sorry, from now on you're just calling them jeans that fit you and jeans that don't, and there will be no need for any more potentially humiliating nomenclature that frankly just draws attention to parts of your body that haven't existed for quite some time, on the no naming, no shaming principle. OK?

Job Ads

Forties job hunters must approach this exercise with the patience of England football supporters and the forensic skills of Hercule Poirot. It's not just that you've been here before, but you know that yours is now the dangerous age as far as employers are concerned. Or, put it like this: when did you last read a job ad that was asking desperately for a person who knows who Susan Hampshire is and can do a mean Barry Manilow karaoke for the office Christmas party? Exactly.

It seems that everything acts against this age-group – from experience (too much and no one knows the vision statements you've seen) and qualifications (too threatening and extensive, and knows how to use a semi-colon) to a general philosophical wisdom that 'delegation' and 'empowerment' are just management-speak for dumping even more work on you.

It's as if many job ads are automatically wired to warn off anyone in their fifth decade. Forty might be the new thirty, but in the recruitment industry it's more likely to be the new sell-by date. In fact, with thirty-five now being suggested as the career acme age, some are wondering if there is actually any point to higher education or working, and wouldn't it be more sensible to go straight from school into gated communities and miss out the boring bit in between?

Anti-age discrimination, it might be claimed, is going some way to remedying this. But all it has really meant is that the recruiters have got subtler and more devious in their ad-speak to warn off anyone who still remembers The Brotherhood of Man.

They say ...	They really mean ...
A fun and dynamic team who live and breathe the brand.	No one has a permanent relationship or proper home life and they like to visit nasty vomitous pubs every night.
Operating at the global interface.	Forget your child's Nativity Plays for the next ten years.
A player with young attitudes.	Er, young.
An energetic approach to your work.	Curl up and die now if you couldn't be the understudy for *Dick and Dom in Da Bungalow*.

Person Friday.	Only the really desperate need apply.
IT literate.	Can't have anyone over forty as you probably won't remember your password, loser.
Definitely looking for the wow factor.	Sorry, not the zzzz factor.

John Lewis

It comes to most of us in the end: a realisation that we only ever wanted to live in a world of limited choice where there are only two types of latte whisk, where nothing will go out of fashion because it was never fashionable in the first place, and where staff don't automatically regard you as a serial shoplifter.

A definite sign of middle age? Turning into one's parents? Not actually caring anymore what one's children say? All of these, probably. But, sorry, it's our life, and we can buy a seriously boring mahogany sideboard if we want to.

K

Kidding Yourself

Living thirty miles and a two-hour commute from a major city still means it's a suburb.

The slippers you bought from M&S are only for occasional use.

You're not actually humming the first three minutes of *The Four Seasons ad nauseam* because you only ever listen to Classic FM.

You didn't really want that promotion.

Claiming that you've turned forty for the fourth time because it sounds less traumatic than forty-three.

You don't possess two (at least) of your parents' most irritating habits.

Having sex once a fortnight because you're both too tired and it's the only time there isn't a child in the bed is merely a temporary blip.

You only saw *Ladies in Lavender* by accident.

You'll write a bestseller soon and will look like Joanna Trollope, only even thinner.

Kidult

Apparently some people in their forties can't accept that they are older and are keen to prolong their youth by behaving as if still adolescent. The retail industry likes to encourage this, of course, as it isn't stupid and wants as many middle-aged men as possible to upgrade their Playstations and think they can't live without a £1,000 toy scooter.

The only known solution is to have a child – or even a

number – to ensure total 'closure'. This way any kidults soon pull themselves together as the benefits of more adult pursuits like not eating food disguised as letters of the alphabet, going to the toilet without the door open and talking proper sentences finally kick in.

L

Land's End

Mysteriously everyone receives this catalogue once they are forty, recognising that by this age people will prefer to try on strange fleece overgarments in the privacy of their own homes and preferably without mirrors. Written in a wholesome prose style, it depicts a world of orgasmic design modifications and exciting extra features.

Land's End is, however, the glamour end of this market, and although, like its lesser rivals, the emphasis is on sub-zero or tropical temperatures – with a concentration on bright colours for mountain rescue purposes – it at least suggests that skiing and yachting, as opposed to rambling and waiting for public transport, may be on the cards for every fortysomething.

In fact there appears to be a recognition that the forties could be a time for fresh activities that until now no one had thought of. This includes a new range of clothing for 'perfectly bridging the gap between living room and bedroom', where winceyette-looking fleece outfits and duvet-warm moccasins enable you to lie dreamily in your hall with your pre-bedroom cup of cocoa and a strange look on your face. If, in your new-found languor, you catch yourself dropping off, then you will need to power-lounge in 'snow-soft' but hygienic Polartic blankets which fortunately inhibit the nightmare growth of odour-causing bacteria, obviously felt to lurk around everyone over forty. Most people like to buy at least one item, the more sophisticated usually going for a velveteen polo neck, so that they can pretend to be Austin Powers with other consenting adults in the privacy of their own back garden.

Late Gap Year

While at one time people in their fifth decade seemed happy to go down the well-tended path to peaceful oblivion, today's more assertive generation isn't going anywhere gently. After twenty-odd years in the workplace and the pressures of bringing up a family, you suddenly realise that you too want a Life Changing Adventure and to collapse on some sand in Thailand thinking you're Leonardo di Caprio in *The Beach*.

Inevitably it will take a fair amount of time, at your age, to convince your corporate employer that 'time out' will be a 'good thing'. After all, you'll need to justify them not paying you for six months and offering your colleagues the pick of your job roles, not forgetting how you'll be 'adding value' to the company and bringing back a whole range of exciting new skills.

Skills you can claim to be bringing back:

- Strategic (I'll have a much better overview of the universe and the place of four-hour petty cash meetings in it).

- Leadership (I'll actually have made my own decisions for once without another bald middle-aged person telling me what to do).

- Empathy (I can sense that everybody thinks I'm having a nervous breakdown, but then what's new – at least I'll have a decent tan).

- Creative (If I haven't thought of an imaginative way to escape this place by the time I get back, I will have failed).

What not to say to corporate employers:

- I want to swim with sharks because they'll be less lethal than you.

- I want to scream into the Samaria Gorge that you're a bunch of f***** shits.

- I want to talk to a monkey because it'll be more stimulating than you.

- I want to attend a voodoo ceremony and make sure I don't forget any of your names.

It's only now you wonder what exactly you're letting yourself in for. You are in your forties after all, and old enough to be the parent of younger Gap Yearers. It is worth remembering, however, that in many developing countries you will be felt to be in the upper echelons age-wise and would normally be an old age pensioner or else dead. Locals will either honour you as an elder as befits your advanced age or try to understand your reasons for travelling across half the world in order to sit on a plastic carrier bag in a tent and eat Snack Pots and tell people about your mild existential crisis as a result of your horrible line manager or how Xmas 2005 with your Surrey relatives brought things to a head. It may be best to say you only wanted a break – just try not to worry whether someone's stolen your hole-punch back in the office or if you're going to end up with the wobbly chair when you finally return.

Later With Jools Holland

Who would have thought that a frankly naff and amateurish format, last seen on *The White Heather Club*, and MC'd by a person who sounds as if he may once have introduced strippers in a Bermondsey pub, would become a lifeline for people in their forties? But how else are you supposed to hear about new music, bearing in mind that your last live concert was probably The Tweenies with several thousand recently continent fans.

And as not every act is in the top twenty (or hit parade, as you like to call it), there's every hope that older children will vacate the room at the mere sight of anyone not pointing to lower parts of their anatomy. Which leaves you free every Friday night to think you're still cutting-edge and have discovered the Klutons before anyone else. Don't mock – it's all that lies between us and Dave Lee Travis.

Leather Trousers

Let everyone know you'll be saving these for your 'I am fifty, alright?' birthday celebrations, just to get this one out of the way. At least it will give them something to look forward to.

Leg Warmers

Er, remember how these looked on you in the eighties, when you were a mere shadow of your current self. Now multiply your previous size by a factor of two at least, and also question if you really want sympathy for chilblains in summer, or whether rainbow might trigger an epileptic condition in your dog.

Life Expectancy

It's all very well thinking that living longer means we can leave lots of annoying tasks for later as there will be plenty of time. But it's now struck many in their forties that all this means is the many things they've put off doing in their thirties they'll have to get around to doing now. These include:

Learning a new signature dish that doesn't involve pasta and one saucepan.

Washing everyone's scarves and gloves.

Putting a new CD in the car CD player.

Opening the car bonnet.

Finding out why the lawn is yellow.

Knowing more about IT than your five-year-old.

Deciding what you do with six perfectly good thermos flasks minus stoppers.

Making a costume for your child's Literacy Hour that isn't a multi-purpose cloak (i.e. dustbin bag).

Joining a gym for longer than one week.

Actually reading flat-pack furniture instructions.

Finding out how long guinea pigs live.

Lifeplan

If we haven't got a lifeplan already, life coaches advise us to get one as soon as possible. Whether this is in addition to the current version that seems to have been written without any co-operation from you, and is already quite exhausting enough, is not very clear. But think very carefully if you really want any more bullet points or exclamation marks in your life at present.

Life Skills

Your children are forever coming home from educational institutions apparently equipped to the hilt with these. At a time in your life when it's easy to feel under assault from all sides, it's good to remind yourself that you too have Life Skills. After all you must have had a life and there must be some perks resulting, mustn't there, so just think positive. Don't let anyone try to convince you otherwise. By simply doing your own Life Skills audit you may be surprised at the fascinating range you've gone and accumulated over the years.

A typical forties life skills profile

Knowing what a teenager is thinking, even though she hasn't spoken for two days.

Knowing what a parent is thinking, even though you haven't spoken to them for two days.

Able to set up a Freeview digital player so that at least you get the Shopping Channel and another which promises adult entertainment (although it never works).

Knowing that if you turn a PC on and off enough times someone more technical than you will eventually point out that you've spilt ice cream and several Jammy Dodgers down your keyboard again.

Able to smile at people you don't know with so much transparency you like to think you might be turning into Mother Theresa.

Able to reach a destination unaided by Sat Nav (mainly because you're unable to use it).

Knowing that shop-bought mince pies always taste exactly the same as the other sort.

Life's Too Short At Forty To ...

By the time you're in your forties you begin to feel, as never before, the brevity of life. It's as if, each time you step outside the front door, there's one of those little planes trailing a message across the sky in front of you: *Tempus Fugit*, it says, as you feel the shadow of the Grim Reaper stitched to your heel like Peter Pan's shadow. (At least it makes a change from what you usually find there.)

It's all part of being a proper grown-up. You may remember Shirley Conran reminding us that 'Life's too short to stuff a mushroom'. Well, now you know it's too short to do lots of other things as well, including:

Hating Jeremy Clarkson.

Bearing a grudge against an inanimate speed camera.

Thinking you are going to live for ever.

Stuffing any vegetables, mushrooms included. Period.

Being sniffy about frozen food.

Blaming it all on your parents.

Still feeling sorry for yourself.

Only dreaming of downshifting.

Making your own filo pastry.

Drying out the teapot.

Digging up your daffodil bulbs on an annual basis.

Knitting gloves.

Bearing a grudge.

Trying to understand MySpace.

Only playing air guitar.

Caring if you embarrass your children.

Watching too much TV and then complaining it's all rubbish.

Trying to train your cat.

Trying to train your partner.

Blaming society for everything.

Starting being sensible now.

Olivia, the fortysomething employee losing her job

Call her a Mid-Life Professional or Mid-Youth, if you really must. Only don't say she's 'X' years old.

Olivia is forty-nine and hopes that it doesn't offend too many delicate sensibilities. She's just heard that her company is in dire financial straits – redundancy rumours – which is why she's now doing what younger people she knows seem to spend every other night doing: working on her CV.

'Don't put your date of birth: 22-year-old recruiters will put you straight in the bin', says one friend. 'But if you don't they'll know straight away that you remember Steeleye Span', says another. Or, thinks Olivia, they could decide the bonkers old person has just forgotten how old she is. Chief executives (male), of course, can be as old as Adam and no one bats an eyelid. So what's new pussycat? Just don't get her started on that one.

Meanwhile she ponders on the extensive career in which she's survived booms, busts and restructurings, and which has revealed to her some eternal truths about corporate life: these are (a) the lower you are in the office pecking order the bigger and (if you are female) more cat-oriented your leaving card; (b) middle-class people who keep their Le Creusets in size order at home think nothing of owning cups with harrowing stains and sharing an office kitchen that makes Mrs Royle's look like a Phillippe Stark; (c) when you come back from holiday your litter bin is always missing; and (d) if management thinks team-building can be encouraged by playing Giant Scalextric, it needs its own batteries examining. The rest is tactful silence.

Of course, she's supposed to be more disciplined and have less time off than younger people. She doesn't feel any need to be defensive about her IT skills – she can download Instant Messaging with the best of them. And she has no problems working with people of any age – if Darren and Emma want to have sex and then others want to let all the G8 countries know about their love knobs with graphic visual reminders, it's up to them.

As for transferable skills, she can't really see what all the fuss is about. She's spent most of her working life doing other people's jobs for them – from MD to distribution. But what she doesn't want yet is her skills transferred to supermarket cash desk, nor to be an early-retiree doomed to a little light Pilates and discussing Louis de Bernières in a reading group.

Will she give in and mention her 'can-do, upbeat youthful attitude' in her CV? And claim that she's only 39? Of course she will. Olivia's not stupid.

Lost

You probably are. You just wish someone would show them the way. Accept that there comes a time in everyone's life when you can get enough po-faced post-modern enigma with associated red herrings before you open your front door, thank you very much.

Lounge Music

'Guantanamera, guajira Guantanamera …'. Forties people have a more fraught relationship to this than they'd have you believe, as it's the kind of music their parents were playing at their age at Black Forest Gateaux dinner parties on a Dansette record-player. It's a little less ironical and retro than they might like, especially if they find themselves singing along a little misty-eyed. In fact, they think they'd rather change the subject if that's alright.

Lying About Your Age

Sorry, claiming you feel ten or that forty is the new thirty on your CV is not going to convince many employers, especially if Andrew Ridgley's shorts are still your main 'special interest'.

M

Madonna

Singlehandedly responsible for making many fortysomething women feel that they should either (a) re-invent themselves or (b) might as well give up now. Whenever anyone in their forties utters the fateful words 'I feel like a lie-down' or 'where's my fleece?', the spectre of fabulously toned kabbalah millionairess Madonna looms to remind them that with just a bit more effort they too could have a number one record and be condemned by the Pope for being publicly crucified.

While many might have expected to find her fifth decade more mellow, she has proved a model to us all by continually metamorphosing herself and her music, while at the same time acquiring more children by whatever means. It's called 'having it all' or 'having a nervous breakdown, if you don't read the small print'. Only we know how tired we're feeling.

The Madonna makeover guide

Madonna	You
Re-inventing yourself.	In your case it might be more realistic just to come up with a new name. Try the telephone directory.
Doing two hours minimum exercise a day.	Time to move on up from getting slightly wet in Aqua Aerobics.
Conversion to Kabbalah Judaism.	You may need to start taking those strange men in black who knock at your door a little more seriously.

Writing children's books.	Of course you are creative. Just look at your CV: it's the biggest fantasy since *The Lord of the Rings*.
Being written off and rising, phoenix-like, yet again.	Whatever your line manager said at your 360 degree appraisal, just tell yourself he's jealous of your PC with its lovely fairy lights that resemble a Mexican peasant shrine.

Male Body Hair

At the first sighting of a fortieth birthday card, most places on the male body make a concerted effort to produce as much hair as possible. 'Where has all this hair come from?', its new owners ask. 'It wasn't here on our thirty-ninth birthday'. Suddenly hair pops up from shirt collars, appears down trousers, peeks out from shirt sleeves, attempts to join eyebrows, and sprouts in unstoppable profusion from ears and nostrils. It is as if overnight each male has decided to audition for a film about the life of Tom Selleck and is eager to provide a rich harvest to make sure the part is theirs.

The full-time job of male grooming now commences in an attempt not to be mistaken for a walking, talking rug. And while the typical man will now have enough back hair, for example, to stuff a sofa, the hairs on his head may be counted in double figures if very lucky.

The balding forties male may be vaguely compensated by the thought that his head hair hasn't actually disappeared: it has just been re-distributed in a socialist way around the rest of his body. It is still there. It just doesn't feel like talking to any of its old friends at present.

Male Earrings

If he's just seen the latest *Pirates of the Caribbean*, and for the third time, be worried, be very worried indeed.

Man Boobs

Just when you thought nothing else could go wrong with your body, along come these strange protuberances popping out of your chest, making you look like an unconvincing trainee Lolita with stubble. Best kept hidden under those big baggy 1980s T-shirts you've had in your wardrobe all these years. You always wondered what you were keeping them for.

Marathons

It's noticeable that as some ambitions fade, others emerge. Which is why at any marathon race you're likely to see a high proportion of people in their forties who until recently have only unsuccessfully run for buses.

Admittedly your age group is in a difficult position as it's neither young nor particularly old, and people will suggest you are having a mid-life crisis under the selfish pretence of raising money for charity. Although, of course, you can't possibly win, and if, as is likely, you collapse dramatically and need to receive medical attention, it won't engender much sympathy but only tut-tutting about drawing attention to yourself and wasting valuable resources. It's what's called another lose-lose situation – but you will probably be used to this.

M&S

Marks & Spencer's recent rumoured demise struck fear into the hearts of many fortysomethings as they contemplated the potential clothes purgatory that lay ahead.

While before only perhaps a minor attraction for the bits that not many people saw (boring but comfortable underwear and socks), Marks & Spencer has now started to loom brighter as an Aladdin's Cave. Because as other shop doors start to close, we were rather hoping to turn to the panacea store where (a) outlandish fashion tendencies are kept firmly at bay; (b) youth and size zeros fortunately never get beyond the pot pourri at the front door; (c) sales assistants are less given to picking at hangnails and blaming us for spoiling their left-footed shoe displays.

Having now brought somebody in to turn it around and do something about the kilts, we are able to feel less guilty about seeing Marks & Spencer as our store of choice. But everyone knows that it hasn't really changed. Any item of clothing may still be grabbed in the knowledge that it will probably fit, can easily be bunged into a washing-machine and will just about distinguish us from an old age pensioner.

Only don't admit to any of this, that's all. Not even to yourself.

Mears, Ray

For some reason, every middle-aged man secretly wants to roast weevils, sleep in a hammock above a 1,000-foot gorge and make a contraption to enable him to drink his own sweat. While admittedly this is more difficult in urban areas, special day survival courses are available to help him test his powers of endurance, break his ankle in a rabbit burrow and get it out of his system.

Melua, Katie

We wouldn't quite call it a dependency situation just yet, but we're getting there.

Menopause, Male

Everyone is allowed to joke about this more than the female version, as most women feel men are only claiming to have it as an excuse not to help in the house and to draw even more attention to themselves. But at least they've given the latter a name this time, which their partners have to admit is quite crafty.

Men's Magazines

They're either just a little embarrassing (puerile sex fantasies for thirteen-year-olds) or boring (puerile sex and car fantasies for thirteen-year-olds). This may suggest that your early *FHM* days of getting excited about the prospect of Gail Porter wearing half a nurse's uniform may be coming to an end. In the meantime, you're still just about able to have an opinion on the size of Jodie Marsh's breasts, but you're not sure for how much longer.

Menopause Conversation, The

Usually a group of women at the back of a health shop looking appalled: does this mean they've really got to spend the next twenty years only eating tofu? They will go deathly quiet whenever a man enters, just in case he thought they might be discussing something else.

Metrosexual

Er, don't worry about it: just do your best with the Old Spice toiletry set your family gave you the Christmas before last.

Middle-aged

Well, are you or aren't you? Put it like this: you're either in denial or you're in very big denial. Never let anybody say you don't have a choice these days.

Middle England

There's an unwritten assumption that by your advanced age you should be a fully signed-up member of this. Membership permits you to have certain inalienable rights and beliefs that are totally non-negotiable and everyone else should abide by them or else you will just have to send Simon Heffer around to give them a good seeing-to.

You are expected to believe that:

- Judi Dench is a national treasure and has never made a bad film or appeared in a duff play.

- *The Antiques Roadshow* says something about your inner psyche.

- Let them tamper with the *Shipping News* over your dead body.

- The BBC is Marxist.

- Jane Austen and *The Vicar of Dibley* are fully signed up members too.

- *My Family* is a situation comedy.

- The State should stop being nanny-like except when it comes to making sure that young people, gays, women and gypsies know that they are only really honorary members of society and should stop making a fuss.

- The Sixties are when Britain's moral decline started.

- Anything else can be explained by mothers going to work.

- If you wave a copy of the *Daily Mail* at someone they will magically understand and apologise for being inadequate.

- You would like to carry around Lynne Truss in your handbag and she should correct the spelling of graffiti artists too while she's at it.

- Ideally the National Trust should take over the running of the country and issue everyone with compulsory scented drawer-liners.

Middle Management

If you're in your forties you're meant to be in middle manage-ment. Unfortunately, faced with *The Office*'s David Brent as the archetypal middle manager, many fortysomethings now feel under tremendous pressure not to resort to any of his behav-ioural traits, lest their teams laugh behind their backs at them even more than usual. These include his typical ways of doing appraisals, motivational speeches and running meetings; in fact anything that involves human interaction and asking people actually to do something productive.

If you manage to get through a year without displaying any of these signs, don't worry, everyone will still be waiting for you to do your David Brent impersonation at the office Christmas party. Please don't disappoint them.

Mid-life Crisis

Changing your career.
Changing your partner.
Changing your appearance.

Changing your car.
Changing your supermarket.
Changing your cat.

If any of these happen at an earlier or later age, they are much less cause for comment. But because you're in your forties they're diagnosed as part of your imminent mid-life crisis.

Remember that from the age of forty any deviation from your usual dreary predictable behaviour and routines will send those close to you, and not so close to you, into paroxysms of merriment as they whisper to each other that 'they told you so' and 'he's not even wearing a mullet or earrings but he's showing all the signs of major personality disorder'. Everyone knows that by the age of forty you're just the sum of your hormones (or what's left of them at the bottom of the jar).

It's important not to over-react, as this only give others further ammunition. But it may be easier just to pretend to break down and claim all Norah Jones's songs are about you. At least it lets everyone know you only ever wanted to be a stereotype and should shut them up.

Mid-youth

Term first coined in the late nineties by editors and marketers who realised that women in their forties didn't have their own magazines to make them feel guilty and suicidal. They were felt to have different lifestyle needs to younger readers, i.e. had all the dieting tips they could cope with and if they read about another dream handbag they were going to scream. However, at the same time they weren't yet ready for knitting patterns or cutting out pictures of cats.

But rather than calling them what most people at forty call themselves, usually 'knackered' or 'tired and emotional', they decided to give them an exciting new feelgood name that no one could quite understand. When, for instance, did they stop being early-youth and when would they be declining into the depressing sounding old-youth? Most fortysomethings decided that, quite honestly, they had better things to do with their time especially when they can read their children's *Heat* magazine to know which failed liposuction operation to giggle at.

Mini-break

Aka child-free zone. The most carefully planned manoeuvre since the Battle of the Bulge for many fortysomethings, and totally not to be confused with the family holiday. Likely to be accompanied by wild fantasies and dreams of doing strange non-child-oriented things that will involve uninterrupted:

1. Sex
2. Reading
3. Adult conversations
4. Meals
5. Urination

Even if the airport is miles from the destination and the people dance in felt national costumes in your hotel foyer, this will not matter. It is enough that no one is telling you what they have done in the toilet or asking you what concrete is, for a minimum of two days.

Mistakes

At our age, of course, there will be an increasing number of these. But how could we ever learn anything if we didn't make any mistakes? It's just that you're not quite sure what you've learnt from them, especially if you've just gone and ruined another Dyson by sucking up the contents of the cat's litter tray again. You'll get the hang of it eventually.

Morrison, Van

Curmudgeonly Irish singer responsible for a lot of out-of-tune and terrible keening, especially when men over forty are in the shower. The sound produced usually resembles something marine that is being put out of its misery but not quickly enough. Might be identified as 'Bright Side of the Road' in a few cases.

Morrissey

For some fortysomething men, still the missing link between Oscar Wilde and God. In the eighties the lyrics of The Smiths gave their sensitive younger selves the courage to do something about their solipsism, finally leave their bedrooms and attend Smiths concerts. Still an adulatory, near-hysterical following of those for whom adulthood never really happened – which is a little worrying to say the least and may give a new meaning to the concept of emotional immaturity.

Mortgage

Er, put it like this, yours in comparison makes the albatross around the Ancient Mariner's neck look like something out of Claire's Accessories.

Motorcycle

Most fortysomething men are much too embarrassed to even look at a Harley Davidson, such are the implications that you (a) are having a mid-life crisis; (b) are in urgent need of Viagra; (c) enjoy touching and admiring other men's gear shafts.

Music Magazines

If anybody when you were young had suggested that in your forties you'd still be avidly reading about the difficult tenth album syndrome of rock musicians, you'd probably have made the biggest 'that's gross' sign possible. But here you are, twenty-five years later, reading about Neil Young, Eric Clapton and Jimi Hendrix, and any other newer upstarts, like Paul Weller and Oasis, who won't make your iPod drop out. *Plus ça change, plus ça* more or less stays exactly the same. Relax: everything else has just been a nasty dream.

The fortysomething will have slowly graduated from the *NME* (mourning the death of punk for twenty years) and *Sounds* (its now defunct embarrassing Spinal Tap version) through *Q Magazine* (when you're much too busy in your thirties to know what you're meant to like, but suppose it should sound like Coldplay) to find themselves in the final Elysian laid back land that is the world of the mature person's music magazine.

It's not that you feel embarrassed reading *Mojo*, *Uncut* or *The Word*. After all, you have to admire them with their once pioneering features on battered and bruised rock icons, rediscovered rock classics and guide to what music today can possibly touch the hems of past rock gods. But is it just you or do new bands or singers always have to sound like the old ones to pass muster? And isn't the mature magazine's music *de nos jours* Americana just a load of country and western clichés sung by manic depressives for the tragically near-hip?

It's like breathing very pure, filtered oxygen where all impurities and nasty things have been conveniently removed. There's just a lingering feeling that your demographic just isn't producing anything surprising any more and the only way forward is back. Of course, your offspring find it embarrassing and if they have to hear again about the sixties, the punk revolution and the way you're strangely silent about the eighties, they think they're going to scream.

Inevitably you might feel like a perpetual teenager and believe you share the same interests in music. But nothing in fact could be further from the truth. No wonder your children prefer to hide out on MySpace and listen to groups with names like The Dayglo Abortions and Weaselpee they know you won't want to mention at dinner parties. You're actually on very different planets. When you break down yet again while listening to Brian Wilson's latest version of 'Smile', remember this: it's you, not them.

The fortysomething–teenager rock translation guide

	You	Them
Franz Ferdinand	Thank God, something that sounds like the early eighties. I can still do air guitar to this. Just.	They were alright in 2004, I suppose.
Bob Dylan	His new album is his best since *Blood on the Tracks*.	Who's he?
HMV	Sorry, how else am I supposed to know anything's been released since New Order?	Er, ever heard of downloading?
Led Zeppelin	You were conceived to 'Stairway to Heaven'.	Eeeeegggghhh.

The Wicker Man	I loved Britt Eckland's breasts.	Didn't you have a girlfriend, dad?
Eric Clapton	God I.	Is he famous?
Morrissey	God II.	Is that the bloke with man breasts?
The Rolling Stones	Gods III.	Isn't one of them in *Pirates of the Caribbean?*
Over-commercialised	I can remember when we would only shop in Rough Trade and everything would go back to their profit-share collective.	Then why are you supporting global capitalism by spending £50 a week in HMV?
Bruce Springsteen	The Boss.	You are sooo embarrassing, let me out of here.

Musical Creep

It's insidious. It's mutationville. It's what happens to the musical tastes of fortysomethings as they find themselves forced down the long and winding road that inevitably ends up in a cul-de-sac called 'nothing I can't hum or don't already know the words to, thanks'.

By the time you reach forty there's every chance you will be having sexual intercourse on a fairly regular basis in a warm environment or else are just rather tired, i.e. you are not a teenager and won't feel quite so sorry for yourself on a 24/7 basis and wish to have someone to remind you by singing about it.

If you have teenagers your partner will be especially pleased by the change, as one group of depressed Goths in the family is definitely quite enough. But it does mean that a lot of music, past or present, is no longer speaking to you about your life. Nor will you be reading *NME* to find out about the latest indie band, listening to illegal radio stations or trawling MySpace to meet your fellow alienated.

Sadly though, it's not quite as easy as this. While your parents always seemed to be singing along to Sacha Distel, yours is a much more uncertain progression. Blame Mick Jagger (note: much older than you) for making you feel you should still be burning with a hard, gem-like flame, but also blame your own generation that can't quite put its rock hero days behind it.

This is why today's fortysomethings have to make some tough decisions. Question: Do we decide not to listen to any-thing recorded after 1988 or else do we decide not to listen to anything that sounds like it wasn't recorded after 1988? Answer: we listen to Franz Ferdinand, The White Stripes, Norah Jones, Katie Melua and Jamie Cullum, have a mildly ironic flirtation with Duran Duran, and thank our lucky stars that the morose singer-songwriters of our youth are back, but are pleased that they seem to have washed their hair this time or don't require us to go on so many tiring demonstrations.

Easy listening? Comfort zone? Still scared of seeming out of date, but feeling definitely post-acne? Of course – just don't tell anybody you're still waiting for Elaine Paige to do her version of 'Pretty Vacant'.

MySpace

Strange parallel world where everyone seems to want to be your friend and where your teenage children like to spend most of their time. Worry after your one and only visit that a person from California will arrive at your front door who wants to share emoticons with you for the rest of your life.

Mythologies

Each generation has its own mythology, it's just unfortunate that yours includes the seventies, the so-called decade that taste forgot, and the eighties, the decade that taste also forgot as well as not knowing how much greed was good enough.

This could lead to low self-esteem for many fortysomethings, for whom other generations always seem to have more exciting and positive mythologies. But do also remember that while, for example, the sixties generation likes to claim it was always having tumultuous sex and burning Wicker Men, a closer look at the evidence suggests most of them were in fact living in suburban cul-de-sacs and having fondue parties. Try and remember this if you ever think you've got a misery memoir coming on.

N

Nativity Plays

In a good year, your child will be a shepherd, leading to spontaneous applause from rows of fortysomething working parents at the massed ranks of John Lewis tea towels on their children's heads. In a bad year, your child will be an angel, which will necessitate an expensive purchasing decision and a lot of guilt that you didn't stick every feather on the wings yourself and refused to cut up your one and only purchase from The White Company.

New Father

No one bats an eyelid at younger fathers, but the fortysomething version will attract more prurient attention, usually implying something along the lines of (a) I didn't know you were still doing it; are you using hydraulic lifts or something?; (b) you're obviously preparing for a poor pension by populating the world with a whole raft of mini-me slaves to see you through your advancing years; (c) shouldn't you have some idea about birth control by now?

Nobel Prize Syndrome

Most scientists and mathematicians peak by their early thirties, so just accept you will probably never receive the Nobel Prize now for your work in Quantum Mechanics. That's one less sleepless night, then.

Normal Behaviour

When your parents were your age, they were expected to

have several pairs of colour-coded slippers and to begin worrying about whether or not they were getting too old to like Harry Secombe. Today many forty-year-olds see themselves as only just beginning, much to the dismay of their own parents and their children, who aren't quite sure what kind of Frankenstein creature has been unwittingly unleashed.

Your children will just have to do their best to help steer you a clear path between finding one suitable item that fits you in Zara and people asking if you are wearing that because you're doing something for Children in Need and would you like a donation?

Nostalgia

Don't worry: nostalgia is a perfectly normal emotion at your age. You are expected to have distinct memories that can be easily triggered by all kinds of things, and may be rich, evocative or embarrassing, although chiefly the latter in your case. It's true that many of your nostalgic memories are from the seventies and eighties, but just see this as terribly bad luck. Remember ...

Blue Peter: Whatever happened to the wonderful world of sticky-backed plastic, advent candle coat-hanger holders and tins with pipe spills? No, please don't tell us – it's too distressing. Or remind us where you were when Petra died.

Smash Hits: Jason. Kylie. Wham. Bananarama. More innocent times when everyone wore bandanas and had pores.

Top of the Pops: Never the same once Pan's People stopped dancing in unsuitable crotch-hugging hot pants made from old curtains, when your dad liked watching.

Family holidays: When everyone went on a package holiday to Spain, while being advised to take water-purifying tablets with them, and brought back bullfighting posters as presents.

Smash: Was it just you, or did Smash always taste more like real potato than the real thing?

Colour spectrum: This seemed simpler too: orange and brown in the seventies, while in the eighties we moved on to neon lime and jaundice lemon.

The Establishment: Remember that? At least people then didn't have any illusions that there was such a thing as a 'classless' society and Che Guevara wasn't advertising Smirnoff.

Feminism: At least when feminists reminded us that it was a 'patriarchal, male-dominated, sexist society' you didn't have to worry about the conundrum of post-feminism and Jordan.

Sex: *The Joy of Sex* made it seem a lot less troublesome, knowing that if you didn't follow the bearded man and the instructions below it would just be about the propagation of the species and something rather biological – as with your parents, of course.

O

Office Birthday Parties

Many people working in offices have been thirty-nine for as long as they can remember. This is hardly surprising, bearing in mind the fear engendered by your official office 'It's the Big One And Time To Lose Whatever Little Credibility You Had Left, Sucker' fortieth birthday celebrations.

Think of the last days of the Marquis de Sade meets Riot in Cell Block 11 and you'll probably have quite a good idea what to expect, and that's just for starters. Bearing in mind that your colleagues are only too happy for any excuse not to work and Grotesque Card and Gift Shop sees a fortieth birthday as the ideal way to get their graphic designer specialising in small sexual organs working overtime, no one can quite believe their luck. Except you, of course.

'The Big One' offers the perfect opportunity for maximum humiliation and embarrassment. While turning thirty in an office is usually a low-key affair, forty only brings out new sadistic depths in everyone around you. It might be the new thirty in the magazines, but the message you're receiving loudly and clearly is: it's all downhill from this point onwards. Your birthday gives everyone the right to pinpoint your failing sexuality, social incompetence, lack of hair and bad fashion sense, just in case there was anything you might have forgotten in moments of your usual low self-esteem.

Once they've got the date, expect your party to be the best-kept secret since the publication date of the next *Harry Potter*. Soon you'll see the person with the worst present taste in your office scurrying around for donations. And don't worry about these being small. This is one of those rare occasions when everyone will want to splash out more than two pence each to ensure your day goes as nauseatingly as possible.

Come the Big Day, expect to see your new age advertised across the organisation and on nearby roundabouts, just in case anyone doesn't already know. But the official start proper begins when a five-foot padded card is hauled into your cubicle and you read as jocularly as possible various obscene messages just to let you know what a lot you have to look forward to.

Then comes the Big Present. The Anne Summers wrapping paper should have warned you that it was going to be a Tickler Set/Bondage starter kit/After dinner willie chocs. Although you're forty, your colleagues would like to pretend you're actually a sexually precocious eleven-year-old with a prurient interest in curry-flavoured sex oils.

Unaccustomed as you are to public speaking, you grit your teeth and tell them what wonderful people they are, how you love them all and how great it is that everyone has such a wonderful sense of humour. Of course, this isn't the end. Because next the 'entertainment' arrives, usually in the form of a pole dancer who, judging by her grudging attitude, is obviously only doing this temporarily while waiting for more exciting brain surgery opportunities to come along. It only takes a few minutes before you're half way up the pole with her, being encouraged to have simulated sex, while she looks at her watch and informs you that you have three minutes left. Drunk colleagues are only too happy to take photographs and send them to everybody in the company and the western industrialised world, while putting your promotion prospects for the next twenty years in a completely new light.

Old

You always like the people who say to you 'forty, that's no age' and 'you're only a nipper', but do remember that they're likely to be at least eighty. You're also very enthusiastic about those who say 'I always thought you were ten years younger' and 'you're kidding'. When you reveal your actual date of birth, you're less keen on those who say 'you're as young as you feel', especially if, as is likely, you're feeling like death warmed up and toasted sunnyside-up because you've been awake all night with a teething baby.

You're even less keen on those who like to remind you how soon you'll be eligible for all the advantages of Saga Insurance and can afford to be run over in style. Always remember, though, that to your children you will seem to be an eternal ninety, while to your parents you're likely to be a perpetual ten. Work out your median age when you're feeling particularly strong.

David and Jan, the fortysomething parents with older child still at home

David and Jan thought that, at the ages of 49 and 47, respectively, thanks to advances in medical science and the end of parental responsibilities, they'd be going on expensive holidays and shopping for ever more in Waitrose. But, alas, this was not to be.

There had, admittedly, been three fairly halcyon years while their son did Sociology and Work Sheets at university, and they paid his fees, gave him an allowance that

---

seemed like something out of *Brideshead Revisited*, and received infrequent visits in return. But they soon got over this – it was the 21st century after all – and there was the compensation of exciting sex in all kinds of unimaginable places around the house and garden, though when people asked if they didn't find it lonely without Justin they remembered to look sad. They loved their son but hadn't missed the moods that were more changeable than the English weather, the horrid indie music and the grubby girlfriends.

Admittedly, it wasn't their son's fault that he had been dealt with so perfunctorily by the university's career advisor – five minutes of treading on people's dreams, to quote Yeats, and the suggestion of teacher training. But to give the latter his due, it was difficult to think of an entry route for someone from south London who was vaguely interested in writing song lyrics but hadn't actually done anything yet. Which is why they can now hear the not very muffled sound of Razorlight thumping down from the ceiling above them. Their son, together with several hundredweight of sound equipment and a student debt equivalent to the GDP of Haiti, is back again.

Apparently in Italy it's quite common for male offspring, to live with their parents, even up to the age of forty. David and Jan try very hard to imagine they're in a classic Italian film that's a cross between *Il Postino* and something by Fellini, but they think the weather must make a difference or maybe it's something do with Catholicism. And they do understand about the astronomically high cost of property and how it's necessary for him to have his washing, cooking and cleaning done free. It's just that there are moments when they wish it was just a teenager up there. Most of his friends are either still at university or working, and the visits he gets are usually from strange people they've never seen before. The next Arctic Monkeys? Drug dealers? Alchemists? They haven't got a clue. But they know that at his age he's too old to be grounded or told to be home by midnight, and soon only the Estonian Spirit of Independence Birch Liquor will be left in their drinks cabinet.

Apart from this, it's just like old times. Their son's as communicative as ever, and when he is, it's to criticise their musical tastes. He sleeps most of the day and pads around his room at night like the mad woman in the attic and seems to blame them for his non-existent attempts at a career. They're building themselves up for a friendly chat about job applications but are anxious to keep the channels of communication and fresh underwear open.

They've put their cruise and ambitious sex life on hold for the time being. They're currently having a size-restricted relationship in the utility room – the only soundproof room in the house – which isn't too bad as long as you remember not to knock over the tumble dryer. At least they know when he has to sign on once a fortnight that the house will be theirs again. They're hoping he might go to Glastonbury later in the year, paid for by them. That'll give them something to look forward to.

One Thousand Classic Films To See Before You Die

Faced with all those TV programmes and books telling you what you should have seen, you're starting to feel quite stressed realising what you haven't done in your first four decades. You do wonder how you've managed to spend quite so much time watching the films of Chuck Norris when he's not even on the list. Why couldn't somebody have told you?

P

Parents

Over forty years later and they still don't understand you. We may love them dearly, but being handed down horrid M&S skirts with pictures of clocks on them on the basis that we're the right size now or having our father sighing at our moon-surface lawn, reminds us that they still don't see us as we like to see ourselves, i.e. twenty-one, wearing a T-shirt that says 'Education Not Missiles' and finding handy household tips in Carlos Castenada.

No matter how hard your parents are trying to turn you into their mini-me, you're still hoping that resistance might not be futile. At your worst you might do parents-lite, but are sensibly avoiding anything involving a complete move into matching velour snooze suits at this stage.

	Parents	**You**
Slippers	Multiple pairs.	They were a Christmas present, honest.
Pensions	The complete package.	Banking on receiving the highest ever bid on e-Bay for your 1978 glam rock platform boots.
Child rearing	Tell children what to do.	Enter into lengthy UN consultation process.
Interior design	Depressing seventies.	Er, non-depressing seventies and of course it's ironic and post-modern.

| Garden | Extension of their being. | Of course we don't mind if you want to say it looks like one gigantic cat's latrine, not really. |
| Baldness | Bald. | Bald. |

Parker, Sarah Jessica

There was something amusing about early middle-aged women in *Sex and the City* wearing Manolo Blahniks and pretending to be ten years younger, except having better fellatio jokes. But Sarah Jessica Parker's film roles now seem to be growing younger every year. We're not asking for folk wisdom at forty or grotesquely positive role models, but we don't think that being on the verge of having a dental brace and developing teenage acne again is helpful, that's all.

Parsons, Tony

If you're in your forties and didn't think yours was a crisis of masculinity or thought you were coping well with a separation or a second family, don't worry, Tony Parsons will soon put you right.

Parties

Is 11.45 pm too early to leave a party or not? Forty-pluses have a whole raft of excuses up their sleeves and should never be ashamed of using them at any time. These include:

The babysitter has to go home.

The au-pair and her boyfriend will be waiting up for us in our bed.

Our toddler likes to watch The Shopping Channel about now.

Our Goth teenager should have done a complete cycle in their Dracula cupboard by now and will be ready for bed.

I have this thing about having to touch everything in my bedroom at twelve o'clock exactly.

The cat gets fractious.

We haven't had an argument yet, and if we include time for the one we always have on the way home, we need to leave now.

Pensions

Most of us will spend a lot of our time worrying about our futures. In the long term, of course, we'll all be dead, but until that happens we're banking on someone actually liking our 1992 Barratt home or else beating the market and finding an investment *gîte* in Uzbekistan.

We all know how good pensions have been for our baby boomer parents. But every fortysomething realises that not only will their retirement age be raised, there might well not even be any retirement, such are the vagaries of house prices, children's education and poor company pension schemes. All most of us can do is keep buying a lottery ticket and hope that our pensions adviser is just being funny.

Personal Philosophy

By your age you should have one of these. Basically, it will suggest that if things hadn't turned out this way, they would have turned out the other, with more than a touch of *que sera*

sera and not forgetting *je ne regrette rien*, and there might be something in *Zen and the Art of Motorcycle Maintenance* if you could only remember what it was.

Personality Traits

By this stage of life you should have some. Despite the best efforts of the education system, employers and your parents, that peculiar and eccentric bunch of nerve endings that is sadly you will have won through. They may not necessarily be what any of you wanted, but are now likely to be set hard and fast in super-glue and no one can take them away from you, no matter how hard they might have tried. Look at it like this: at least they're yours and yours alone, and it's too late now to blame them on (a) society; (b) God; (c) listening to the Grateful Dead while smoking old dried banana skins.

Of course, you still don't know whether to feel flattered when people say you don't just have personality traits but Strong Personality Traits, i.e. do they really mean you're a pig-headed and unreconstructed old git who won't listen to a word anyone else says? All you can do is worry about your children's genetic inheritance and hope they don't start getting any ideas.

Pizza Express

Favourite restaurant for fortysomethings, although rarely by choice. Many hoped they'd put their student days of penurious 'Fiorentina pizza, please' eating behind them, but rising mort-gages and growing families with children unable to eat anything that might have come from a natural source soon put paid to that. Had a mild flirtation with Pizza Hut, until your children saw the salad bar.

Plastic Surgery

Refusing to go gently into that good night at one time involved finally being yourself, or, if you had no original ideas, wearing purple and eating three pounds of sausages in one go. Now, it's generally done in private and is more likely to involve a visit to a plastic surgeon.

You know you're ready for plastic surgery when the botox consultant has a fit of giggles as you ask if you really need any work and couldn't you just carry on with your usual cleansing regime. But the pressures of competition from a younger generation, whether at work or in your relationship, together with a media where no one must look older than twelve, finally persuades you. This is decided on the basis that 'it's for you', of course. No one believes this, but is hardly going to say 'I'm insecure, with feelings of low self-esteem', at least not until they look in the mirror and can see that their plastic surgeon was trained by Michael Jackson's.

Work colleagues are obliged never to admit to noticing you've had plastic surgery, although they are allowed to say that you 'look fantastic'. This allows your radical transformation and strange bug-eyed stretched look to be accounted for by a fortnight away or by a very long dental appointment. If your real age wasn't very clear before, at least they now know to put a Greatest Seventies Hits Ever CD for you in the Secret Santa, just in case anyone had forgotten.

Priorities

As you get older, it's inevitable that priorities will change. When you were younger, you were probably selfish and ego-tistical as you were always attempting to satisfy your own needs. The arrival of a family means that you need to think about other people for once, and this will probably involve (a) knowing every glottal stop in the DVD of Mary Poppins; (b) driving a car that Jeremy Clarkson has declared a fatwa against because you need to transport the equivalent of half your home everyday; (c) having a Crazy Frog ring tone on your phone, even though you find it totally nauseating and embarrassing in meetings because someone under ten persuaded you. Of course, no one told you about this – they didn't want you doing a runner.

Property

If you aren't a member of the property-owning classes by the time you're forty, everyone will feel jealous and wonder why you should be exempt from serious indebtedness for the rest of your life and living among people for whom lawns and *Cupressus leylandii* are an extension of their own pubic regions.

Prozac

Everyone either starts looking at you whenever this is mentioned, or else discreetly looks away sympathetically, as if this might be an area you won't want to be reminded about too much at present.

Pullovers

Sorry, only to be worn by Dick in the Famous Five.

Punk

The mere mention of spitting people wearing bondage suits with safety pins and razor blades, and leaving a cheerful message of nihilism, is enough to bring a lump to the throat of many fortysomething men. The birth of punk is seen as an iconic moment in their lives, when they were glad to be alive, with everything that followed an inevitable sell-out and disappointment. Their partners expect to be seen as part of the post-punk let down, but feel it would be nice if other fall girls and guys could perhaps be arranged just once in a while.

Q

Questions, Questions

Do you look with passion at the picture of a woman in a special bath in one of those ads at the back of the *Daily Telegraph Magazine*, except the lust is only for the bath?

Is everyone being reluctant to ask you how you are because they know you'll only want to tell them about your bad back?

Do you ever wonder what's happened to Keith Chegwin?

Are you having to buy a new wardrobe to keep all your fleeces in?

Do you say you have a deep and intense relationship with animals because they understand you and don't talk back?

Can you say, without irony, that you've heard how Madeira is like Torquay, except with more palm trees and donkeys?

Are you actually looking forward to a new series of *My Family*?

Do you secretly worry you'll never find a pair of slippers as comfortable as those you're currently wearing and that look like a couple of recently run-over furry animals.

Yes, we thought so.

R

Radio 2

It's been a long and winding trajectory from Loved-Up Raver Who Thought Acid House Would Solve the World's Psychic Malaise to person in smelly festival tent who dreams of fluffy white towels, a mini-bar and a toilet they can actually sit on. But that's where you are now, so bow graciously to the inevitable.

In your darkest hour, be honest, you secretly feel a little ashamed that you (a) can't tell the difference between garage and rap (and isn't listening to music played by people who wear hoods and frequently feel their genitals only encouraging your children?); (b) have recently enjoyed reading a sixteen-page article in *Mojo* on 'Crosby, Stills and Nash: The Next Fifty Years'; (c) only heard of José Gonzalez because of the car advert; (d) think MySpace is a reference to your on-going parking dispute with the local council.

As for the zeitgeist, you really don't wish to hear anyone talking about this again, thank you very much. You've had more zeitgeists in your time than Victoria Beckham has had hair extensions, and they were all tiring and usually involved you worrying for hours over the right shade of grunge brown to wear to a Health and Safety time bomb ticking away under Acton High Street that called itself a 'club'.

Thanks to Radio 2 you can breathe a sigh of relief that you no longer have to decipher and pretend to like the latest cutting-edge sounds. The nice people at Britain's most popular music station have gone out there and selected all the tunes you already know most of the words to. OK, you realise this means groups that sound like someone you saw on *Top of the Pops* when you were fifteen, along with misery fest singer-songwriters still feeling suicidal after all these years, but at least you haven't completely slipped off the known universe into the slough of Easy Listening despond. Not quite.

They've even – oh frabjous day: and this is your guiltiest secret ever – chosen those eighties singers and songs that sum up the hopes and fears of your formative decade – er, the one that proper instruments and the more tasteful combinations of the colour spectrum forgot. At least you can now go the whole hog and do a karaoke to Bonnie Tyler and feel completely beyond the pale, along with eight million other people.

Of course, there's the ever-present fear that you're listening to a radio station your parents always seemed to have on at your age. You might claim to like Franz Ferdinand but, yes, you're turning into your parents and are only ever a listings away from *The Organist Entertains* and a detailed tribute to Cliff Richard's Bachelor Boy years. Fortunately, though, Radio 2 did a demographics check, worked out that its listeners were dropping off like flies and brought in new presenters. You might have moved from Generation X to trainee member of Generation Zzzzz, but it somehow makes it less embarrassing when Jonathan Ross (47) plays The Clash, reminds you that Mick Jagger is old enough to be your grandfather, and says 'wanker' on air. You can still have irony and edge: you just don't want to be in a mosh pit exchanging body fluids with someone you've never met before.

Don't think of it as giving in. More as exploring all available options and deciding you prefer the one marked 'I'm passing my Velvet Underground records on to the next generation and I happen to like J-Cloths.' It comes to us all.

And just to convince yourself that age discrimination isn't all it's made out to be, you can always work out just how much

Jonathan Ross is getting paid per second. At least you know who to blame.

Radio 4

Dangerously tempting for every fortysomething, especially if you find yourself (a) listening to a programme about British vegetables and secretly enjoying it; (b) apoplectic with rage when *Quote Unquote* is under threat again; (c) enjoying realistic afternoon plays about old people who befriend runaway punk rocker drug addicts.

No one expects you to be listening to an illegal pirate radio station from a Walthamstow sub-let council flat, but you may wish to do something before paralysis of the radio knobs finally sets in and you can only listen to *Quote Unquote* or something with Gyles Brandreth in it.

Regrets

You've either had a few or you regret nothing. The jury's still out. Don't think anyone's trying to rush you, but they do wish you'd make up your mind as consistency is important, and if you're not careful they might start getting a little bit irritated. Incidentally, your major philosophical pronouncements are much better made under non-alcoholic circumstances, especially if after ten minutes of karaoke you're doing those strange movements that are your impression of a rock star, and are next letting everyone know that 'You Make Me Feel Like Dancing'. Anyone under forty should look away now.

Retirement

Sorry, you've got miles to go before you can sleep on a day

bed recliner and know who the hair stylist supervisor is in *Diagnosis Murder*. You don't even want to think about it.

Tom, the redundant fortysomething

If someone had told Tom that, at the age of 47, he'd be sitting in an industrial estate outside Milton Keynes being asked to define his aims and objectives, he wouldn't have believed them.

Of course, Human Resources had tried very hard not to say that he was fired. The redundancy word had been kept to a minimum. But he was in his forties and there were a lot of younger people in the company and he was presumably expensive. Had someone noticed how he wasn't actually addicted to secret (*sic*) BlackBerry use in meetings? Was he a little too laid back at the last Away Day? Had they noticed how he'd learned to say something stupid at the start of every thought shower session and then had a snooze?

He'd have no trouble finding a new post with all his excellent skills and qualifications, they'd told him, as if redundancy was offering him a genuinely exciting opportunity. He tried to be as professional as possible. He excused himself and locked himself in the toilet and did a breathing exercise – or did he just mean tried to breathe? The person who informed him of senior management's decision and offered him a thoughtfully provided biggie sack (for the personal possessions he'd be taking home with him next day) was fifteen years younger than him.

Which is why Tom is now sitting on a chair in front of a woman called Miriam. She had been selected as his personal life coach as part of his package. He was prepared to go with this for the time being and, in any case, his company was paying. She was about his own age and had been recommended 'for her listening skills'. He thought she might have wanted to be a gipsy at some stage in her life, as bangles and a billowing yellow skirt made her resemble a walking, talking solar panel on a drab day in January. At least she smiled all the time. It made a change from everyone else, who gave the impression of being in the vicinity of a minor road accident.

Miriam also talked about exciting opportunities a lot (he counted 24 opportunities and 17 excitings). Then she mentioned entrepreneurship, self-employment, creativity and hobbies, and finally ended a little too quickly with economising. There was even a suggestion that he could become a life coach himself being possessed, like her, of substantial life experience. They obviously didn't anticipate anyone his age actually finding another proper job, he thought. Only if she was so good at defining her aims and objectives, what was Miriam doing discussing his not very interesting future in a converted garage outside Milton Keynes? He hadn't the heart to tell Miriam that this wasn't his first outplacement session since he was forty. She was just one of a number of Miriams who came along offering aromatherapy and limitless horizons, together with a generous range of financial packages. The important thing, he knew, was for him to appear imperturbable and slightly enigmatic. He didn't want anyone to get the wrong idea and accuse him of making a career – or did he mean a non-career? – out of it. He wouldn't like anyone to think he wasn't taking it seriously.

Rock Festivals

To go or not to go? This is the dilemma that faces many people your age as the festival season beckons. On the one hand, this could be the last time you'll ever get to stand in a field in the middle of nowhere, wearing a tie-died Celtic shirt, and singing to yourself. On the other, there's a difference between dad-dancing in the privacy of your own bedroom and doing it in front of 70,000 people who thought they had come to see Kasabian.

Fortunately, many of us manage to find a solution to this problem: it's called our children. They're always asking to attend a rock festival and it will also be an ideal opportunity for you to pass on all the exciting rock festival lore you have garnered over the years. Besides which, as you inform them proudly, you know the words to 'Wonderwall'.

In return, they can make sure you're slightly less embarrassing than might otherwise have been the case by not letting you wear a rainbow-patterned jumper that makes you look like a children's entertainer from Devizes. And don't forget how it will give you a certain *je ne sais quoi* among your work colleagues. They thought you were just a dreary corporate drone and now you're going to prove them all wrong by eating a magic mushroom and having a psychosis about evil druids and flying saucers for the next ten years.

It's as if the intervening years just fall away, as you make your neighbours a peace sign, bib, and tell them you're on a Journey. Eighty miles up the M4, to be precise. There, but for a challenging hair follicle situation and advanced waist size, goes your twenty-year-old self. How did you ever manage to work in systems processing for all those years?

During the journey, you regale your offspring with tales of the legendary performances, alternative communities and once meeting someone who had met someone who'd met Bob Dylan. They look at you slightly appalled, but can't tell you to shut up as you're paying for the tickets.

There's that unforgettable smell of hot dogs and patchouli, and so far you only appear to be the twelfth oldest person on the festival site. But, as you tell your children, it's not camping as you remember it – what's this? hot water and toilets? – and the fact that a mobile phone company is the main sponsor only brings out the ranting socialist in you. They didn't have celebrity tents in your day – even Marianne Faithful did her pills in a cow field just like everyone else.

Then comes the music. Is it just you or is it terribly loud? You're sure it wasn't quite this volume when you last saw Hawkwind greeting the dawn with an extended hurdy gurdy solo. And why is everyone talking throughout when they have presumably paid as much money for tickets as you? Fortunately for your children, you have agreed that they can go off by themselves, provided they text you every two minutes to let you know that they are still alive.

You start doing a peculiar dance not seen since the re-run of Pan's People's gyrations to David Bowie's 'TVC15' on *TOTP2*. No one wants to go near you in case you're dangerous. The woman from the St John's Ambulance Brigade gives you a more than cursory look.

Where have you been all these years? You never wish to leave this place. You feel for the first time in ages that you are breathing properly, if a little too quickly. You remind yourself that you're only 48 once.

But then you have an acid reflux attack and are taken to the first aid tent where you text your children. They come to collect you, ask if they can have all your Pink Floyd LPs and your 1978 army trench coat and can you put it in writing before you die.

You have been told …

Wearing fairy wings and a net dress with a pair of Doc Martens is not a good look for anyone over four. Ditto any item of clothing that makes you resemble half a sheep, unless you want to be mistaken for a Blue Peter presenter from 1983 who hasn't been able to adjust.

Anyone your age or older still performing does so under an invisible banner that says: 'isn't it wonderful we can still play without a life-support machine?'

If you really must, take off twenty air guitar years from your real age, but you don't have to let everybody know.

Stop telling everyone you're on a Journey because at your age, let's face it, it's probably going to be from your tent to the toilet and back again in the middle of the night. Watch the guy ropes.

Keep your colourful array of tablets away from impression-able youth – they'll only discover these are for a range of embarrassing bodily conditions best summed up as 'gross'.

Check your level of profanity – no one wishes to be told charmingly that listening to you is 'like hearing your grand-parent say fuck.'

Give youth a chance to have its own nostalgia: you're only young and trying not to sit on a filthy latrine and thinking it's romantic once.

Role Models

William Hague
Adrian Mole
Boy George
Boris Johnson
Tom Cruise
Mick Hucknall
Sindy
Barbie
We know ...

Roller Blading

Sometimes confused with roller skating until it's too late and you're lying underneath several dozen other participants who are trying to think of a way of calling you an idiotic old turd without making it sound ageist.

Rolling Stones

A combined age of over 250 years. Multiple world tours. Every member at least ten years older than you. Let this be the last time you complain about exhaustion and only being able to slob out watching another rubbish ITV series starring Lisa Tarbuck. Feel guilty, feel very guilty.

Ross, Jonathan

Often held up as the benchmark and ur-standard for this age

group. While Michael Parkinson on his TV chat show is reckoned to be old and sycophantic, Jonathan Ross offers edge, bleeped-out words and better gag writers, plus an exhausting range of other TV projects. His radio show has even made Radio 2 dangerously near-hip and made everyone forgive them for Bob Harris. Some fortysomethings secretly wonder though if he isn't too much of a tough act to follow for the rest of us and couldn't he occasionally be seen to fall asleep and ask what day it is too?

Round Robins

What oft was thought and never well-expressed. Please don't think that just because you're now forty you have to show off and let all your friends and relatives know in nauseating detail everything that you and your family have achieved. It will only encourage them to do the same, except with even more GCSE passes. Maybe better to just send your normal 'robin in desolate snowscene' Christmas card and wish everyone peace and prosperity without itemising your own family's personal contribution to it. But if you really feel you must ...

What every fortysomething circular letter should contain:

- Number of record-breaking exam passes by your children, preferably achieved at least two years before their peers.

- Children's extra-curricular activities have now entered triple figures, including their on-going correspondence with Stephen Hawking pointing out logical flaws in *A Brief History of Time*.

- How both partners have been extensively promoted, received huge bonuses and are being groomed for their Boards.

- Pets have been identified as bordering on genius level and dog is studying for degree in Quantum Mechanics.

- Family went on several highly educational holidays, together with minute accounts of every meal eaten.

- Garden has appeared in *Evening Standard's House and Garden* and has been suggested for the next Chelsea Flower Show.

- Partner still has time to weave old supermarket bags into smocks that Sienna Miller has expressed an interest in.

- Family visited 97 cathedrals in 2007.

S

Saga

Excuse me, you can't be nearly that age, you think, as the first Saga insurance brochure, aka The Reality Principle, plops through your letter-box. And what kind of Big Brother-like database do they have to know that you will soon be leaving the shores of mid-youth for the unknown waters ahead? Have you really reached the age when everyday a different animal charity will be offering you a free biro? Yes. It suddenly hits us. We're approaching the Year Zero of fifty.

Saga rage goes through various stages, from being in denial, to fear and loathing, to a final muted acceptance of your imminent fiftyness and the advantages of cheap car insurance and travel.

But, sorry, er, your parents read *Saga magazine*. For the first time in your life, you're now seen as sharing their demographic with them. Surely there must be some terrible mistake? But no, it's perfectly true. There's no point in thinking you aren't eligible, because you soon will be. Welcome to the first day of the rest of your life – just be grim and bear it.

Sanatogen Tonic Wines

Originally prescribed for the days when forty was thought to be a time of terminal decline, *crises de nerves* and lots of lie downs. Today's fortysomethings, who are expected to take everything in their stride – mainly because everyone else is relying on them – are only allowed to be mildly jealous.

Self-Employment

Once you've reached your forties it's a sad fact that employment options start looking decidedly dodgy. That's why more and more of us are encouraged to take the bull by the horns and, aided by a visit to Ikea's home office department and a spending spree in Staples, find ourselves sitting at our brand new desks wondering if we haven't made a terrible mistake as we recall the halcyon days of being paid to do our on-line shopping and to sleep in meetings.

There are many useful books on working from home – but they tend to avoid certain uncomfortable truths.

The A–Z of the forties home aloner

Appearance

Well, just look at you: slopping around in your jeans doing a little light e-mailing. That's what you think: it'll soon dawn on you that, unless you're power-dressed and wearing enough perfume or after-shave to seriously damage the ozone layer, no one will take you seriously. Not even yourself.

Bedroom

Do you really want to spend a lifetime re-creating Virginia Andrews' *Flowers in the Attic* as you pad around a bedroom = sorry, office = in your slippers?

Cats

Cats, once happy to grub around outside while you were out at work, will now meow plaintively and claw at your window, like Cathy in *Wuthering Heights*. Passers-by make loud comments about the RSPCA.

Dogs

Also perturbed by your new daylight appearances on their territory...

Enigmas

Tele-working will mean you won't know your clients' favourite colours/personal relationships/lucky Lottery numbers/glove compartment contents. You'll wonder what picture they have of you – then again, perhaps you'd rather not know.

Front door

Whatever you do, don't open it – you'll only end up talking to a can't-believe-his-luck Mormon or finally meet your gas meter reader.

Gossip

Deprived of office gossip, you may find yourself becoming abnormally interested in your partner's boring work colleagues – a pathetic junkie's second-hand fix.

Home

In a real office everyone works with a common aim – at home, when you emerge grim-faced from your so-called office, you'll find others grazing comatose in front of *Ready Steady Cook* demanding to know why you're not feeding them their five-a-day veg like the Government says proper parents should.

Instant nostalgia

All-of-a-sudden, once irritating colleagues will appear pleasantly eccentric; over-reaching management just victims of the system. You really gave this up just to be on first-name terms with all your call centre operatives?

Jealousy

You will feel that every client on the phone just knows you're sitting on a hideous, purple quilt that looks like something worn by Abba's Agnetha in 1977. This can induce 'real office' envy very quickly.

Keyboard
If you're not slumped in front of one for twelve hours a day – a prime candidate for RSI – then you must be the new part-timer.

Lonely
You may have solved your 'people problem', but only through enforced solitary confinement. But don't worry – the cat will try to cheer you up by meowing down the chimney in Dolby Sound.

Motivation
At 'proper work' (as you come to think of it), you could always read the company's mission statement if you were desperate for a laugh. Now you'll stare at the pile of red bills, have another cup of coffee and remember how you were once commended in a cycling-proficiency test.

New Age
Working from home is frequently hyped as the New Age environmentally sustainable solution for every fortysomething. But you soon discover that it just gives a new lease of life to Freeman's catalogue reps.

Online
Don't let on all you have is an old pc and a fax that has funny turns. It's automatically assumed by your client base that you'll be bristling with technology: feel marginalised because you can't even have a proper 'systems breakdown'.

Phone
Business phonecalls will always come at the wrong moment.

In the office you could always claim to be 'in a meeting'. But now you can't, and saying: 'sorry, I'm just dealing with a dirty Pampers' doesn't have quite that same self-importance.

Quest
Even if your small business is deeply unsuccessful, you must still look on it as a journey of self-transformation – although your bank manager may find it difficult to see this as a reason for extending your loan.

Real office
Always try to pretend you've got one and that there's not really a giant Cabbage Patch doll staring at you from the spare bed.

Small Businessman's Club (*sic*)
Not always what you'd expect. And why would you want to network with a dog shampooist, a person who makes hand-made birthday cards or a trainee aromatherapist, any-way?

Training
Look back with yearning at all those useless training courses you attended. But just think of all the extra time you'll be able to spend, yes, overworking.

Umbilical cord
Try to resist the urge to visit your former work-place. It's exhausting being the repository of ex-colleagues' hopes and dreams – remember that they have no intention of putting their pensions on the line – and keeping up the required level of expected ecstasy over your own hard-won free-dom. If it all becomes too much, gently remind them that they might just have the chance to experience your exciting new lifestyle first-hand – at the next takeover.

Vision
You soon believe that if you somehow acquired a cottage in Suffolk, a vegetable plot, a deep freeze and a bad telephone line, they wouldn't be able to get at you. Work on it.

Workaholic
See how your work-rate will soar, without colleagues' interruptions. Can you actually be over-productive?

X-Files, The
Er, reserved for all the boring letters from the Inland Revenue you keep putting off.

Yuletide
A lonely time of year for the self-employed – even the dreaded office Christmas party takes on a Pickwickian glamour. All you can do is display the handmade card from the woman at the small businessman's club – and hope she doesn't really want to 'touch base' in the New Year.

Zzzzz
Sorry, you haven't got time to sleep. Do you think you're in a meeting with your line manager or something?

Self-esteem

Do you see *Desperate Housewives* as the acme of a perfect forties lifestyle and feel devastated that your boring existence can never aspire to Wisteria Lane's glittering heights? Or do you simply see it as another clever US TV soap that's nothing more than an ironical *Dallas* that has boosted botox shares the world over? Between this Scylla and Charybdis lies the no man's land of forties self-esteem and only you know in which unchartered bog you're currently drowning.

Simon and the second family syndrome

Simon is on his second family and doesn't quite know what's hit him. Although over the head with a heavy mallet might be one way of describing it.

Now in his late forties, he has only dim recollections of his first children as babies. It did seem as if a lot more was done behind screens then, like a takeaway pizza parlour where all was safely delivered in the end. He seems to remember wife number one stayed in hospital for ages and the men were kept out of the way as much as possible. He had had to dissuade his new one from having a home birthing pool and burying the placenta in the garden.

He remembers talking to his original offspring, of course; he said good morning and was perfectly nice to them when he wasn't at work. But it was nothing like the bonding malarkey they expect of everyone today. Is it just him or is everyone more anxious and paranoid about everything to do with children? This time there wasn't just a birthing plan but the baby seemed to have an action plan too and a list of its Kumon tutors from day one. He thinks everyone started getting needs in about 1988. He's taken two weeks' paternity leave and feels terribly modern.

He's getting used to having vomit all over him, as he's trying very hard to be a Modern Parent. His three other children, twelve, fourteen and eighteen, all love Jessica, their new sister, but do find it slightly embarrassing and like to giggle and ask him what it feels like to be up there with Rod Stewart. He doesn't actually find this very amusing as (a) he's not sixty; (b) his wife isn't a lingerie model; (c) she isn't a trophy wife either and has a career in computer accounts management.

As for the tiredness and the nights without sleep, he'd rather not think about it. Not that he actually could. He's too exhausted. His wife is currently asleep and he's sitting up with a squawking head inside a pair of Pampers trying to get it interested in the sale of Joan Rivers's earrings on The Shopping Channel. He's going with the flow. He doesn't seem to have much choice at the moment. They'll probably stick to the one, he thinks, and he's already making enquiries about a non-reversible-there's-no-way-José-and-the first-cut-had-better-be-the-deepest vasectomy. He won't be discussing it with his wife. At least he can blame it on his age. He hasn't told anyone the hospital had asked him if he was the baby's grandfather. He doesn't think that will be happening again.

Senior Moments

Are they or aren't they? One of our greatest fears is thinking that just because we can't remember something means we're on the path to planet ga-ga. If we can't remember where we left our credit card, is that just the next step to the teapot in the fridge? Are we on a fast track to mental meltdown if we once drove our packed lunch to work on top of our car bonnet?

Fortysomethings should be reassured that due to the complicated, multi-tasking nature of our lives, it's not surprising if we are occasionally forgetful. After all, there are only a certain number of things you can do at any one time and most of us are simply doing too many. Think of your brain as an early Amstrad computer that wasn't designed to cope with so many functions and certainly not to remember the difference between a vision and a mission statement. Don't be too hard on yourself, then, the next time the young person on the other end of the line sighs audibly when you can't remember your password; there are still several million permutations and you know you'll get there eventually.

Seventies

It was bad enough surviving the original seventies; now you're supposed to go into ecstasies at the latest seventies revival. This puts you in a dilemma: do you politely say that I had enough of those horrid colours and lava lamps the first time around, or cut your losses and let everyone know how retro and stylish they are? Because for many fortysomethings the seventies revival is like saying 'come on, let's relive my depressing adolescence in a front room in Kidderminster' or 'I really used to love the Crossroads Motel reception area with its psychedelic bile carpet and feel it is part of my inner psyche.' It wasn't an attractive look then, and is likely to lead to even more suicidal tendencies now. Only you know if you really want to have to spend half your total life living in a set from *Abigail's Party* and trying not to giggle when callow younger people ask if you want to fondue. Just hope against hope that it's not going to be stripped pine next.

Sex

Naturally you may not be doing it quite as frequently as you did when you were a student with only an occasional essay crisis to keep you detumescent. Work and family life all take their toll. But bear in mind the mantra 'quality not quantity', so that at least you'll be able to worry even more = especially if you tell your partner this and they try not to split their sides laughing.

Sheds

If a man doesn't have a shed by the time he's forty, tongues may start wagging. A shed suggests moral uprightness and also a continuity with previous generations, a reminder that his father and his father before him all had these 'men's rooms', where they could be alone with dead onions.

No matter how small his garden shed, it will announce to the world 'I am a real man and I'm not afraid of spiders or unidentified creepy crawlies. Please excuse the drying road kill.'

Even the most feminist of males will find themselves getting shed-obsessed and feeling embarrassed about the sudden need to collect old jam jars. But it is, after all, merely a middle-aged development of the boyhood den, a place for self-discovery and masculine affirmation, where a man can be a man unhindered by such social constructs as hand-washing, tetanus injections and not whistling the only bit of 'I Was Kaiser Bill's Batman' you can remember. What this says about the crisis of masculinity, or whether this is the crisis of masculinity, is, of course, a sore point that leaves most shed commentators arguing until the nasty feral cats that somehow manage to get in there come home.

However, just as fortysomething women feel they can't compete with their mothers in the domestic sphere, so their partners can't but help feel their sheds are severely lacking compared with their fathers'. While the latter always seemed to be cutting up corms (the fortysomething man isn't sure what these are and it's too late to ask now) or smoking a pipe and either whittling or banging on a piece of wood, his son just feels inadequate trying to super-glue someone's flip-flop.

The truth is that this generation has seen a crisis of sheds and no one is quite sure what they are for any more. After all, in one's father's day, it would be an admission of masculine failure that you just kept a few 'bits and pieces' there or actually couldn't remember what was in there at all. There is a feeling that the great shed days of yore are over and that what remains is a mere simulacrum, a yet empty vessel waiting to be filled again.

This is not surprising when the typical fortysomething shed owner, under pressure, will reveal his shed to contain:

Pieces of string of various lengths hanging from the roof because they might be useful one day.

A lawn mower that doesn't work.

A croquet box without anything in it.

A ridiculous number of plastic flowers.

Various dead pets' accoutrements.

Printers that don't work.

Various opened tins of paint in colours no one ever remembers using.

Sad remnants of unsuccessful DIY projects that he's meaning to return to one day when he has time.

Ten years' worth of gardening magazines (unopened birthday subscription from parents).

Of course, none of these must ever be moved or touched by other people. Not that members of his family would ever wish to visit his shed, although they are admittedly puzzled by what he does there in the dark (there is no electricity). Fortysomething women, of course, don't have sheds to keep their embarrassing bits and pieces in; they just have very big bottomless handbags. Though whether it would be able to contain a tortoise that may (or may not) be in very deep hibernation inside a Cookeen Lard box is a moot point indeed.

Fortysomething men not expected to have sheds

Peter Mandelson
John Galliano
David Furnish
Tom Cruise
Graham Norton
George Michael

Sixties

Annoyingly just out of your radar, as people only a little older are always smugly reminding you. Yes, you know you missed out on:

1. Legendary pop music.
2. Unlimited sex.
3. Having a psychedelic experience.
4. Wearing flowers in your hair.

And they always like to tell you, even more annoyingly, that if you can remember the sixties you probably weren't there (as you were probably only just there, you wonder desperately whether this might give you a kind of honorary status).

They can only pity you with all your cultural, political and social influences from the dreary seventies:

1. Arthur Scargill
2. Pickets
3. Inflation
4. Harold Wilson
5. The Bay City Rollers

All you can do is apologise for your date of conception and promise them that it won't happen again.

Small Talk

Remember when you were young and used to wonder about the length of time your parents would spend talking for hours on end with others about absolutely nothing of the remotest interest? Well, somewhere around your 39th birthday that will be you.

But look at it like this: you're no longer scary looking, have an obvious attitude problem or a need to wear a T-shirt that says 'Piss Off Morons'. It's why you'll find most people will want to talk to you about (a) the weather; (b) the traffic; (c) the bad behaviour of children; (d) Christmas. It doesn't matter that (a) we live in a maritime climate and rain is always a statistical possibility; (b) the M25 is likely to have a number of cars on it; (c) children will sadly feel a need to speak from time to time; (d) it happens every year on 25 December.

Your co-conversationalist will expect you to reply in a way that is repetitive, non-controversial and a brain-dead experience for all concerned. It's called phatic communication. That means it isn't exactly going to add to the sum of human knowledge and anyone who wants to discuss the Theory of Relativity should probably commit *hara-kiri* right now. It's meant to be boring and tedious and predictable, as every fortysomething knows.

Yes, like it or not, most people now see you as a nice, safe middle-aged person who would like you – and this is scary – to be their friend. But it's worth remembering that while engaged in small talk it's unlikely they'll want to mug or do anything seriously anti-social to you. It's reckoned to oil the wheels of civilisation and suggests life still has time for a few pleasantries. Look at it like this: a conversation outside the Colosseum in Ancient Rome about how Lupercalia was getting more commercial every year and going to the dogs was presumably a Good Thing, as at least it meant Attila the Hun was doing his unpleasant business somewhere else. Try and smile nicely please.

Socialising with Colleagues

Amazingly, most people over forty actually have home lives and don't really want to sit in a boring bar with colleagues after work (a) getting drunk; (b) doing a gangsta rap conga on a Tuesday evening; (c) realising that colleagues are like the new relatives – you didn't choose them and haven't got much in common.

Spring

You may cry a little when you see that an old dead bulb you threw out in the autumn has somehow miraculously survived and bloomed – others toss up whether this is a mid-life crisis, a new season of *Gardener's World* has started or it's where you buried Kylie the goldfish I–XVI without telling the children.

Stand-ups

Is it just you, or are stand-up comedians growing increasingly exhausting – manic, self-obsessed, always angry, in a state of perpetual adolescence and obsessed with their penises? Do they in fact sound quite like your children and don't you deserve a break from this just once in a while? Only you know the level of your tolerance for a moaning person in their twenties having another psychodrama. The Edinburgh Festival is now your idea of hell – you know you're getting too old when you don't want anyone to shout at you anymore and, quite honestly, you'd rather look in a kilt shop.

Step-parents

An increasing number of us find ourselves becoming step-parents. One school of thought, from the Brothers Grimm to the *Daily Mail*, likes to attribute every child problem under the sun to us, without ever appreciating the major effect we have on family life, e.g. wasn't Cinderella's step-mother just preparing her for a sensible career in the service industries?

It does seem unfair for poor step-parents to always take the blame. This is especially the case when they have exponentially increased the number of available guilt-ridden Christmas presents and made any offers of tangerines in silver foil and a lecture on how you were happy with just an old box to play in completely unacceptable.

Stoicism

And you didn't think there was a name for taking a child to the toilet twenty-five times in one morning because they're frightened of the poo monster, be honest?

Suburbia

We all remember the Pet Shop Boys singing 'You can't hide, run with the dogs tonight in Suburbia' and said we were never going back there. It was where our parents lived and people did things like having Neighbourhood Watch meetings, swept up leaves obsessively, and multi-culturalism meant buying a non-green pepper. But it's our spiritual home and where most of us live now. Depressing, we know, but this is real life, we tell any remaining friends still loft-living and doing minimalism, and you try shopping for Pampers in Canary Wharf, aka what have we done to deserve this?

Sudoku

Many over-forties worry that their brains aren't what they were and decide to remedy this by taking up the Japanese number puzzle. But whether drawing attention to their mental decline with strange goggle-eyed looks and mutterings to themselves on public transport, coupled with breaking down and screaming 'I've got it!' exactly convinces others that they still have a mind is not entirely clear.

T

Technology

You probably go back quite a long way here – admit it: you used to play Chuckie Egg on that Amstrad 951 in your first office. Although you can vaguely hack it for simple faults, in the event of anything major, you know to ask a teenager who will always be able to hit a few keys, sigh morosely, and solve your problem in seconds. Ditto your office IT person, who will also like to suggest that you're either a person with very big fingers or must have recently had sex on your keyboard.

Teenagers

Remember it is more difficult for them than it was for you at their age. While your parents were properly grown-up, the chances are that when it comes to music, clothes and even sex (er, you won't want to go there, right), you have a lot more in common and even want to be their friends. How annoying is that for your teen, who wants to be seriously alienated? Many of us still like to think of ourselves as teenagers except with big mortgage responsibilities and more serious nostril hair. This inevitably results in a number of mixed, not to say confusing, messages for everyone concerned.

> 'We'd rather you and your partner had separate rooms because, er, we thought she might like her own Holly Hobby duvet.'

> 'Of course we're not agreeing with your grandparents over extensive body piercing. We're just worried about how long it will take you to get through security and spoil your Gap Year.'

'Because higher education gives you more options in life, including the options that mummy and daddy and your future employers, that is true, would prefer.'

'Naturally dad and I slept together before we were married. It's just that we did it as part of our protest against the military-industrial complex.'

'We love the idea of Serge Gainsbourg, we just don't want you bringing someone like him home with you. '

'We agree Christmas is nothing but a horrid consumer festival, but it is granny and grandpa's consumer festival.'

'There's nothing wrong with a T-shirt that says "Nobody Knows I'm a Lesbian" and a pink kilt that lights up. But not for your auntie's wedding in Godalming.'

'We want you to do whatever you want with your life, as long as it doesn't involve (a) rock music; (b) playing football; (c) visiting Camden Town without live CCTV coverage we can access from our computer.'

'It's lovely you want to do Media Studies, but couldn't you just watch more TV for a bit then study something more useful?'

'We don't really object to Kate Moss and Pete Doherty. We just like the idea of frequent dental flossing.'

'I know I went to my first festival when I was sixteen without my parents, but there were only nice soft drugs then whose effects were designed by the person who did the Pink Floyd LP covers.'

Thermos Flask

Fortysomethings, according to their children, have an embarrassing tendency to draw attention to themselves and in the Thermos Flask may have found their number one must-have *objet d'embarrassment*.

This has probably been one of your best recent investments and, quite honestly, you can't imagine how you've managed to survive without one. Just think of all those years you've been caught short in a crowded public place without a flask of steaming hot tomato soup for everyone to look enviously at? You have finally attained the Age of Reason and decided you'll no longer pay a fortune in Starbucks and have an irritating *barista* giving you their mocha knowledge when you can sit outside on a public bench with your very own *café latte grande*-sized with soya milk at a fraction of the cost.

If you don't mind the comments from passers-by and can close your ears to the hysterical laughter on the other side of the Starbucks window, you should enjoy it.

Things Can Only Get Worse

It's easy to feel depressed in your forties and to think that everything's going downhill. Younger members of the family will deny this and say it's 'just you', but reassure yourself that downhill is in fact the case and some things actually have got worse over the last twenty years.

ITV
Your workload
Woody Allen films
Michael Jackson
People's manners

Universities
US foreign policy
Rich–poor divide
Young people
Exam standards
Booker Prize winners
Madonna
Live Aid
Star Wars films
Channel 4
Glastonbury Festival
Post office queues

There are also some things that have got much, much worse, of course, like your appearance: you may agree with Wittgenstein that whereof one cannot speak, thereof one must be silent and hope everyone else does too.

Thirties

You may have felt very slight tendencies in your twenties, but it's only by your thirties that your 'inner avuncular' may have started to kick in and you'll know if you'll soon be settling into a mellow middle age or wondering if Simon Heffer isn't still a bit too young to make Serious Pronouncements about the moral health of the nation.

Thirtysomething	Fortysomething
Enjoying Russell Brand on E4.	Enjoying Russell Brand on Radio 2.
A little birdie says that you could do with a good detox.	A little birdie says that you could do with a good botox.

Attending an over-25s disco out of interest.	Attending an over-25s disco out of desperation.
Four weddings and a funeral.	Having lost count, quite honestly.
Meeting your friends and discovering new music on MySpace.	Asking your child what you have to do and if it's legal at your age.
The years when you finally pay off your student loan.	The years when you think you'll never pay off your mortgage loan.
Blaming the over-forties for having all the good jobs.	Blaming the under-forties for wanting to take yours.
Energy.	Conservation.
Remembering that Cézanne was well into his thirties when he first attracted public acclaim.	Remembering that Van Gogh was already dead when he first attracted public acclaim.
Having the hopes and dreams of youth.	Having a Lottery scratch card.
Someone shouting 'Party! Party!'	Someone shouting 'Baby-sitter, Pampers, bleeper.'
Sturm und Drang.	*Vorpsprung durch Technik.*

Time Out

Do you say: (a) I'll read it next week; (b) Oh, God, I think it's in the cat's litter tray; (c) Do I really want to be sitting in a room above a pub in the Archway while a Chilean theatre group does experimental things with a Brechtian sub-text and worry about muggers on the way home?

U

University

Thanks to the post-war education boom, your generation has more people with a university education than ever before. It is now far enough away for most of us to have nostalgic memories of Marxist lecturers in leather jackets who had epistemologies (*sic*), CND stickers, the smell of Vesta Beef Curry, and sex in chaste narrow beds – while also knowing that today, in any emergency, you can always write a 2,000 word essay.

While sometimes wondering if your degree ever actually equipped you for anything more than discussing The Great Corn Law Reform Bill or John Donne's later poetry, you will nonetheless wish to encourage your offspring to take advantage of all available educational opportunities. Exchanges like the following can be heard up and down the country between forties parents and their teenage children:

You: Why did I find your UCAS form in the recycling bin?

Young Person: (Mumble) Because I don't want to go to university.

You: But you need a degree more than ever nowadays. People with A Levels are doing the jobs that used to be done by those with O Levels. Though, of course, your mother and I have always encouraged you to take responsibility for your own decisions.

Young Person: So, I'm allowed to make my own choice?

You: Yes – no.

Young Person: Are you saying that three years of studying something I'm not very interested in and a student debt of £40,000 is going to help me in the future? Someone in my school left after Year 11 to run a market stall selling Russian watches and now he's a millionaire.

You: Er, you have to think of it in the long term. It's about transferable skills — and a love of your subject.

Young Person: You told me you only did English because it was easy and so you could look up girls' skirts during lectures.

You: But look at how it's benefited me.

Young Person: What, looking at girls' knickers?

You: It's given me choices in life.

Young Person: You mean, you didn't actually have to be a Quality Evaluation Manager?

You: You could always have a Gap Year and live in a very undeveloped place on very little money to find out how most people survive.

Young Person: Wouldn't it be easier if I just stayed in my bedroom and did the same thing?

You: How about you do Creative Writing with Subsidiary Plumbing Studies Just in Case, we pay your fees and keep you in And You Will Know Us By The Trail of the Dead CDs for the next three years?

Young Person: I'll think about it.

University Alumni Society, The

In general, successfully resisted by most graduates for many years on the basis that 'that was then, this is now' and mixed memories of a university course that equipped you for work life with a vague understanding of terminal moraines. For some unknown reason, you're regularly sent the alumni news which only makes you realise that jobs for life still exist (dear old Professor Muggins still researching Tudor dustbins) and, as part of a marketing push, offers you mugs, key rings and scarves with the university insignia, making you realise how far removed from the global economy, bless, academia continues to be. It also provides opportunities for some graduates to unretchingly let others know about their dynamic career progression, and how they're holding the best Tupperware Parties in Paraguay.

But eventually the alumni society lets you know about a major reunion of your year. You're faced with an existential choice: it's the halfway up the stairs point in your life and if you don't attend now you know you probably never will. But at the same time there's the dread that no one will recognise you/everyone will be more successful than you/everyone's original annoying qualities will now be multiplied to the nth degree/you'll still be remembered as the person who wore purple loon pants. You pull yourself together, put on your best professional demeanour and decide to face yet another fortysomething rite of passage.

But it's never quite as gruesome as you imagine. Of course, it's slightly embarrassing; you may have stayed in touch with some university friends, but probably not your entire hall of residence's tiddlywinks team, who seem to have been in a state of high mutual dependence since 1983. You meet people you haven't seen for years, exchange some addresses, promise to keep in touch and, er, buy every key ring and nylon T-shirt available. It's your alumni reunion party after all, and you can wonder if you shouldn't have done research and eaten Prawn Snack Pots for another three years and sigh nostalgically if you want to.

University Challenge

For the time-poor, intellectually insecure fortysomething, *University Challenge* is often the only window left for you to prove to yourself and your family that three years of university education weren't in vain and successfully equipped you to shout out all the wrong answers at Jeremy Paxman. As your children sit appalled at your sad behaviour, the thought strikes you that if you are trying to make a case for university education, this may not be it.

Unofficial Job Roles

Congratulations. Age and experience finally make you an invaluable member of the team. You might not have made it to the ranks of senior management, but the fact that only you seem to know when it's a false fire alarm and how to produce a classic, infallible sickie makes you a person much in demand.

Of course, you may initially be a little sniffy about your new job roles: are they saying that you obviously have extra time on your hands and your other brilliant attributes don't really matter? They are, but prefer to look at it as a perk of having survived so many redundancy rounds, secure in the knowledge that with age comes wisdom and a desk full of sales conference biscuits dating back seventeen years.

Medical adviser: As the only person who has stayed in the job long enough to vaguely know the contents of the first aid cupboard, you're the one they'll turn to whenever they want to bleed over someone. Fortunately your advice is always the same: take a paracetamol and wear a funny-shaped Elastoplast. This always seems to work.

Career mentor: Having seen your company downsize, re-engineer and outsource over the years, you can provide a benign and mature perspective on the ups and downs of the corporate life to younger colleagues, aka have they ever considered safer options like swimming with man-eating crocodiles?

Relationship counsellor: Through the fruits of bitter experience you are able to advise that today's long hours culture often results in unsuitable office romances. Your hard-won wisdom allows you to point out that it will either be someone you work with or the person who works in the late night garage: it just depends how attracted you are to barbecue briquettes.

Office guru: Only you know where the spare toilet rolls are kept. This is enough for most people.

V

Valentine's Day

It's not that most fortysomethings aren't romantic, it's just that their relationship has probably gone beyond a pink teddy with a Valentine's bib or an Executive Botty Scratcher in a gift presentation case. This also includes those horrible bunches of blue flowers from Nasty Shop that says 'sorry, I forgot again, darling', just in case there are still any fortysomething men who haven't discovered the surprise mini-break.

Vanity

Welcome to the decade where you're reduced to having just one favourite mirror, even if this is rather a strange relationship which can involve you approaching it at a special angle and then only in a certain light. This mirror has become your best friend because it always flatters you, will never tell you the honest truth or talk back and only remembers the good times. Although it is rather a one-sided relationship, whereby you only want to receive positive news, it seems to suit you both and has withstood the test of time. You have had tarnished relationships with all the other mirrors in your life and there is obviously something seriously wrong with them.

Viagra

Is it just you, or are email ads for cheap Viagra popping into your inbox with hideous frequency? How do they know your age? Are they trying to tell you something? Why do they always spell it 'erekshun'? How many does your work colleague get? And are his bigger than yours? All these questions need answering. And fast.

Francesca, the very reluctant grandmother

After her divorce (she doesn't actually need to work any more but likes to call herself an interior decorator — chiefly of her own home), Francesca decided to re-invent herself. For the first time in her life she could afford to. She brought in a posse of helpers and advisers to re-brand 'own brand plc' as the self-help books tell you to do.

She had a new hairstyle, her life coach gave her advice on her innermost needs and whether she could afford Heals furniture, her personal trainer worked her out, and her plastic surgeon said he was only gilding the lily during her eight-hour operation. She thought it would all be plain sailing, provided she didn't smile too much.

Then she heard from her daughter. Emma had a perfectly good job and wonderful opportunities and then got herself pregnant accidentally. It wasn't fair. Mother and daughter were meant to go on shopping trips together with everyone mistaking them for sisters. What had Francesca done to deserve this?

When she mentioned her daughter's predicament to her life coach he went all ga ga and asked if she would be knitting a matinee jacket. This wasn't what she wanted to hear. She could feel herself looking at least 42 already. She was still young and vibrant. She had worked so hard keeping in touch, watching boxed sets of 24 so that she would have something to say to people under thirty-five. She hadn't planned on being a grandmother until she was 88 and was ready to go silver-grey and wear her hair in a bun.

Rory was a plump and gurgling baby who didn't look like anybody they knew. Francesca let her daughter know that she would be much too busy to look after the baby and Emma agreed. She knew her mother. Of course, Francesca had had her daughter at the same age, but that was then and this was now. Everyone knew you had your children as late as possible as part of your Life Plan, and if this didn't happen or you couldn't face it, then you did what Madonna did and had them flown in.

She should have known it would happen. The baby was ill and couldn't go to nursery school and her daughter had an important meeting. She couldn't say no. It was only right, she supposed. Her daughter was eternally grateful.

Francesca cancelled her day spa appointment. Rory was asleep in his buggy battle bus as she pushed him and half a ton of Pampers, change of clothes and feed, trudging through the streets of SW1. Almost immediately, she met a woman she barely knew and hadn't seen for ages. The woman looked admiringly, but also enviously, at Rory, and said that motherhood was obviously suiting Francesca, and that she had no idea. Francesca had to agree and found it oddly arousing that the woman even thought she had a sex life. Grandmother and grandson carried on and attracted a whole gallery of further admiring looks from passers-by. It wasn't part of her Life Plan, but why hadn't she thought of it before, she asked herself, performing an impromptu Pampers change behind a tree in Kensington Gardens, why hadn't she ever thought of it before …

Vinyl Collection, Your

Aka how embarrassing is embarrassing? While they are rarely played, and most recordings are now available as CDs, the typical owner feels a strange umbilical bond with their collection and may be unwilling to part with it. Whether this is because the range of records could, quite frankly, be used as a witness for the prosecution in any investigation of your psyche over the last thirty years, no one wishes to explore too deeply. Apart from your children's occasional foray to stare at Jimi Hendrix's *Electric Ladyland* cover ('er, yes, there are 68 naked ladies, but this was before I met mummy') and to steal a Curved Air album cover for use as a non-cigarette ashtray, it has been left, Marie Celeste-like, a ghostly and dusty memorial to the sad, distant days of 33 rpm.

Some of us would simply not feel happy for a dealer to make a paltry offer for what have, after all, been the formative influences on our lives. Our first youthful rebellions are here, as are our post-punk reality checks and the electronica that got us through the eighties. We are admittedly a little more self-conscious having seen the anorak record collector in *High Fidelity* – but at least we seem to have mislaid our copy of *John Denver's Greatest Hits*.

Virtual Social Networks

You still can't quite get your head around the idea of spending hours on line in a spooky parallel world of global virtual 'friends', where everyone wants to hang out and stay chilled and remain as enigmatic and annoying to anyone over sixteen as possible. Sorry, it's fewer inter-connections you want, not more. They're just too exhausting.

Volunteers

Some see volunteering as the new Prozac. Because most are well over forty – younger people are either busy working or totally exhausted, poor things – the 'voluntary sector' is the one area of life where anyone your age is seen as ridiculously youthful. The only problem is that you will usually be given the most energetic jobs that no one else wants to do, like swimming in the North Sea in December to draw attention to global warming.

But don't feel too guilty if you're not part of an official volunteering organisation: by the time you're in your forties, such things are an inescapable part of your everyday life anyway as you find yourself:

- Making late night mercy dashes to rescue the vulnerable (picking up children from late night parties).

- Unpaid marriage counsellor (to your friends).

- Animal sanctuary worker (your children have found another ill cat that's about to be put to sleep and thought you might like to look after it).

- Visiting old people on a regular basis (aka your parents and relatives).

- Running regular reminiscence workshops (ditto).

If you really have time to save the planet and reorganise the world's food supply on top of this, think of it as an added bonus.

Waits, Tom

The thinking fortysomething man's Keith Richards. Ex-alcoholic and drug addict and formerly dissolute singer who may be used as a sad benchmark, e.g. 'Would Tom Waits be asked to empty the bins and/or queue up with other commuters for his annual season ticket?', by which your own life may be found to be sadly lacking.

Water-cooler Moment, Having a

Along with many other work-related phenomena beloved by management, most people in their forties now realise that these, sadly, don't exist. It's not that we haven't tried hanging around our company's water-cooler waiting for that Eureka! moment or hoping a colleague might have one we can copy.

Having watched programmes like *Ally McBeal* and *The West Wing*, in which these dynamic power discussions always take place there, it's come as a great disappointment to us that the best we can muster are comradely time checks about how much longer there is to go, or else a discussion about whether it's really tap water. Most of our water-cooler moments now seem to go something like this and we are only too happy to provide a more mature perspective on things:

Young person: Do you come here often?

You: Oh, about six times a day. I'm trying to do my two litres.

Young person: Did you watch *EastEnders* last night?

You: No. Did you?

Young person: No.

You: I haven't seen it since Grant or the other one was murdered. Or was he just injured so that Ross Kemp could leave the series but come back any time he wanted?

Young person: Do you think we're having a water-cooler moment?

You: Er, I suppose we might be warming up to one; sort of like in a training course when they ask you what your favourite vegetable is before everyone slinks into a huddle at the back of the room.

Young person: Do you think management might get rid of it if we don't have at least one water-cooler moment? After all, that's why they're here, isn't it? I'm worried that it might come up in my appraisal.

You: Are you?

Young person: Aren't we supposed to bond synergistically and then have all sorts of blue sky thoughts that will save the company millions of pounds?

You: So they say.

Young person: Couldn't we just have a quick one?

You: So that we can go back to saying it's only 256 days to Christmas and wondering why they use those strange pointy cups you can't put down anywhere.

Young person: I'd never thought of that – about the cups.

You: No one expects you to, at your age.

Young person: So we are having a water-cooler moment, then?

You: You said it.

Young person: I'll mention it at my appraisal. My manager will be pleased.

You: Trust anyone over forty to help you, we know about these things.

Young person: Wow, this could have come straight out of Edward de Bono with the aim of transforming the workplace.

You: I know.

Weight

Only you know about the strange symbiotic relationship you have with your favourite pair of scales. Leave body mass index for a day when there's a 'z' in the month.

Well-known Fortysomething Characters in Fiction

Reginald Perrin.

Wicker Man, The

Everyone now racks their brains as to whether they found this iconic and legendary at the time, or if all they can remember are Britt Eckland's breasts and pubes? It may be six of one and half a dozen of the other, so to speak.

Wisdom

Thinking back to our youth, we all remember those middle-aged aunts and uncles who always seemed to have something wise and intelligent to say based on their life experience, and how it helped for some reason if they smoked a pipe or had nicely comforting grey hair. While a younger version of you may have been impetuous and rude, you wonder if you should be more like this, going for a relaxed but loaded with life-enhancing aphorisms Jean de Florette meets Zorba the Greek advanced role model. This means that, when a colleague accuses you of stealing her stapler and taking it on holiday to bury on the beach, at least you are able to put it into perspective, remind her that her name was on it in big letters, and not scream immediately.

X

Xmas

Fortysomething women, seeing Xmas largely kept alive by their mothers and other elderly female relatives, dread the time when they'll be expected to take on that particular role. Can they really face a future that condemns them to spending eight months of the year sourcing pine cones with cotton wool and hoarding bottles of bubble bath? They can only hope that by the time it's their turn, Christmas will have responded to consumer demand and become a purely M&S-run event with tumultuous scenes of mass worshipping at the turkey truffle butter chill cabinet.

Y

You Wish You'd Known This at Twenty

- Odd socks usually pair up eventually.

- Odd boyfriends and girlfriends usually pair up eventually.

- Having a family Volvo doesn't mean the sky will fall down, although it will mean you will probably have four years of unpacked camping equipment in the back and enough dog toys to start a small circus.

- There's not a lot to compare between sitting in an All Bar One with colleagues after work and being at home with your children, as both will involve copious amounts of vomit and a conversation that you have heard many times before.

- You can have children and read a book once in a while, even if it's only an old and smelly *Captain Hornblower* that someone accidentally left in a holiday cottage.

- Not having sex for a week won't mean that it will get atrophied.

- It's OK to smile automatically at people with buggies.

- Wearing a white jacket doesn't necessarily mean you want to look like Mick Hucknall. It just means you grabbed the first thing you could find in the wardrobe, so no need for the amateur dramatics, OK.

- Kurt Cobain and Courtney Love weren't the best parental role models after all.

- Tracksuit bottoms have elasticated waists for good reasons.

- Having sex with the same person for longer than ten years doesn't necessarily mean that you've failed and like wearing very old pyjamas.

- The person in charge of a training course always calls him or herself a facilitator so that they won't have to take responsibility for all the rubbish that they're talking about.

- Just because you don't know what Bebo.com is doesn't mean you're a failure. Necessarily.

- Shakespeare probably said it all somewhere.

Young Writers

If you're still worried that you're running out of time to make the Booker Shortlist and compete against Zadie Smith, it's worth reminding yourself that writers are still seen as 'young' up to their mid-forties. This, incidentally, makes the author of *On Beauty* about three in real writing years, but don't let this worry you too much.

Younger Friends

If we don't want botox or plastic surgery, and lest we become stale or boring, having younger friends is the latest recommendation to keep us youthful.

The only problem is that we already have a number of younger colleagues at work, but being sent an email of nude freefall Australian parachutists that freezes on your pc isn't most people's idea of friendship. It suddenly strikes us that we haven't got a clue what we're actually meant to talk to them about anyway. Our attempts to play the Neil Young Songbook at home when no one is listening? The amusing irony that we wore the original version of their dress in 1984? It reminds us why the idea of talking to ourselves becomes more attractive once we hit forty. At least we know our favourite topics of conversation, aren't appalled that we don't know how to use our iPod and don't care who eats maggots on *I'm A Celebrity, Get Me Out Of Here*.

Younger Wife

If you're her partner, get ready for people to wink at you: it must be your money, because it certainly can't be anything else. If you're the wife, you must be a trophy version, and people will query why you're still working and not living in a Spanish-Ranchero-Georgian mansion insulated by your expensive WAGS handbag collection.

Youth Phrases

Oh My God … And I'm like … Excuse me … Whatever. Think of how annoying these are whenever your children use them. Now imagine them when spoken by someone over forty with a rising, trying-desperately-hard-to-be-Californian intonation who seems to think they're Paris Hilton. Exactly. So don't. It's, like, So Seriously Grosstastic.

Youthful

A good day is one where someone compliments you about your age and says they thought you were ten years younger. However, you need to check if they (a) want something; (b) assume you have had plastic surgery; (c) have a major sight problem. But as compliments grow thinner on the ground, you may just decide to take it in the best way possible, i.e. lie on your back, scream YES! and burst into tears before asking them to say it all over again please.

Yummy Mummies

Faced with a choice between carrying on working and child-birth, many until now childless fortysomethings will choose the latter, mainly because it involves marginally less screaming. Those able to stay at home, despite possibly having an au-pair or nanny and a lot of expensive spa treatment, dislike being called idle as they face a lot of stress wondering if their baby's first words will be in Estonian. If you continue working, you won't be a yummy mummy; in fact you won't even feel like a member of the human race and may be excused membership for the duration so that no unfair comparisons can be made. Aka dummy mummy.

Z

Zeitgeist

Er, it went that-a-way.

Ziggy Stardust

Not a good look then, and definitely not now. Warning: if you go dressed as him to your fortieth birthday party, people are going to think you're even more psychotic and weird than you really are. Don't encourage them.

Zzzzz, Generation

Forget Generation X, yours just basically wants to go to bed for two months, ideally with low-level flu, and the complete boxed sets of *The Sopranos*, *The West Wing* and *Curb Your Enthusiasm* please.

Making Time

Steve Taylor

Why does time seem to speed
up as we get older? Why does
time fly when we're having fun,
or drag when we're bored or
anxious?

Steve Taylor examines these
questions in *Making Time*,
setting out five basic laws of
psychological time. The result is
an astounding insight into why
our perception of time changes
– and how we can take charge of time in our own lives.

Using evidence from modern physics and his own research into
unusual experiences of time, Taylor argues that our normal sense
of time is an illusion created by our minds. He cites numerous
experiences of time passing slowly – exploring childhood, drugs
and hypnosis, accidents and emergencies, meditation, 'spiritual'
experiences, sportspeople who are 'in the Zone' and some of the
world's indigenous peoples.

In modern society, we've come to see time as the enemy – as
something that's always racing away from us. Meanwhile, we
spend too much of it focusing on the past and the future.

Making Time shows us, on a practical level, how to control our
sense of time, effectively increasing the length and quality of our
lives. But perhaps most importantly, it shows us how we can
reclaim what is ultimately the only thing that we have: the present.

ISBN: 978-1840468-26-7 • Hardback £12.99

50 Facts that Should Change the World

Emma Hartley

'Provides proof of why we cannot be complacent about the world as it is today. Should become the bible of political activists everywhere.' *New Statesman*

'Fearless and compelling. You need to know what's in this book.' *Monica Ali*

- Landmines kill or main at least one person every hour

- Brazil has more Avon ladies than members of its armed services

- A third of the world's obese people live in the developing world

In this brand new edition of her bestseller, Jessica Williams tests the temperature of our world – and diagnoses a malaise with some shocking symptoms.

Get the facts but also the human side of the story on the world's hunger, poverty, material and emotional deprivation; its human rights abuses and unimaginable wealth; the unstoppable rise of consumerism, mental illness, the drugs trade, corruption, gun culture, the abuse of our environment and more.

The prognosis might look bleak, yet there is hope, Williams argues – and it's down to us to act now to change things.

ISBN: 978-1840468-46-5 • Paperback £8.99

Did David Hasselhoff End The Cold War?

Emma Hartley

'Emma Hartley wants to reignite the debate about Europe, focusing on the quirks that genuinely interest us, and the commonalities that unite us. It's a clever ploy she pulls off with aplomb.'
Independent on Sunday

'Europe, boring? It's anything but, according to Emma Hartley's 'wonderful portrait of contemporary Europe.' *Good Book Guide*

- Without Islam, Europe wouldn't exist

- There are half a million semi-automatic machine guns in Swiss homes

- Forty per cent of homes in Romania don't have running water

From the railway in Hungary run entirely by children to the British comedy sketch, unknown in the UK but watched by millions across Europe every New Year's Eve, Emma Hartley reveals the idiosyncrasies and absurdities of Europe today. Covering everything from poverty to pop music via politics and pirates (and of course the Knight Rider himself), *Did David Hasselhoff End the Cold War?* paints a picture of an astonishingly varied continent.

Find out where the worst place in Europe is, why Germans are required to pay a tax direct to the Church – unless they declare themselves unbelievers – and what the twelve stars on the EU flag actually represent.

ISBN: 978-1840467-94-9 • Paperback £7.99

Crunch Time

Adrian Monck and Mike Hanley

'This book appealed immediately. Mike Hanley (an Australian journalist) and Adrian Monck (a British journalist) discuss issues such as globalism, corporate power, emails, the environment and security in an uplifting, inspiring and witty way.'
Sydney Morning Herald

Two award-winning journalists argue about the impact of our unthinking everyday actions on the future of our planet.

Every age and every generation thinks it's special, that it's on the cusp of something big. This time it's true. What we do now will make or break the future.

The problem is that the things that we do every day – drive to work, buy toys for our kids, prepare our meals, have a cup of coffee – are conspiring to break it. Terrorism, poverty, ecological meltdown, climate change, pandemics – this is the background noise we have all learnt to live with. But what if all these things could be laid at our own feet? What if our civilisation is structurally, tragically flawed? What if we are using up tomorrow today?

In *Crunch Time*, journalists Adrian Monck and Mike Hanley argue passionately with each other about the causes of these issues and what we can do about them. Believing that living in the 21st century means being answerable to the future, they help us to understand the critical decisions that we can make now if we want to leave anything of value to future generations.

ISBN: 978-1840468-01-4 • Hardback £9.99

New World Order

Dixe Wills

Nation states – you've got to have them, I suppose. But how much do we actually know about them? If you were drugged, blindfolded and parachuted into a foreign country, would you know you were in Belgium merely by picking up a handful of soil and tossing it into the air?

And nation shall rise against nation.
And the nation with most words for 'moustache' shall win.

If not, it's about time you read *New World Order*, the guide that cuts through the piffle to nail down the essence of every single country on the planet. Say goodbye to sleepless nights fretting over the average number of *puls* to the *Afghani*, or wondering what's in Bhutan today and whether it will still be fresh by the time you get it home.

With a handy grading system to revel who are the globe's real top nations and which ones are letting the side down on a monumental scale, it's no wonder that experts are declaring *New World Order* the most important book to be written in the last 500 years. Without it, all is chaos and anarchy. And that's a bad thing apparently.

ISBN: 978-1840468-10-6 • Hardback £9.99

Wholly Irresponsible Experiments

Sean Connolly

For the little boy in every father, here's the chance to unleash the forces of nature. *Do* try these at home!

'That's the trouble with the real world. Too many people grow up. They forget. They don't remember what it's like to be twelve years old.' So said Walt Disney. How many fathers have felt that way but then just shrugged and returned to the 'real world'? How many would, deep inside, want to release the little boy inside and let rip?

Wholly Irresponsible Experiments offers a chance to do just that. Scores of experiments take you through a dazzling array of not just snaps, crackles and pops, but oozes, crashes, booms and stinks. Irresponsible – maybe. Cracking fun – definitely! Each experiment is clearly explained, with ingredients, methods, warnings and outcomes. Lively illustrations let you see what's in store.

And for those of you who still might feel a little guilty about all of this mayhem, the book includes some handy scientific 'excuses'. The child screeching across the room propelled by a fire extinguisher is, after all, demonstrating Newton's Third Law of Motion. That bit of King Edward potato launched from a tube and ricocheting around the kitchen – simple: Boyle's Law!

ISBN: 978-1840468-12-0 • Hardback £9.99

I Hate the Office

Malcolm Burgess

A dark, edgy yet laugh-out-loud A to Z of the absurdities and horrors of corporate life, from the pages of London's *Metro* newspaper.

Who, when they were six years old, ever said, 'Hey, I want to spend forty years of my life wondering what value-added knowledge capital is in a size-restricted cubicle surrounded by people who watch *Bargain Hunt*'?

Office workers of the world unite!

What makes the 9.00–5.30 sentence quite so gruesome? Office escapee Malcolm Burgess offers a painfully hilarious A to Z of reasons why the office has become the modern byword for servitude.

From the agony of the Away Day via hot desking, office politics, romance and parties, to the sheer terror of work reunions or conference calls, Burgess vents his spleen on the working week.

Ending with the unique Corporate Bullshit Detector, *I Hate the Office* is every stressed-out worker's essential weapon in the war against the angst of modern life.

ISBN: 978-1840467-79-6 • Hardback £9.99

500 Reasons Why...

I Hate The Office

Malcolm Burgess